Essential Histories

The First World War (3)

The Western Front 1917–1918

D1158504

Essential Histories

The First World War (3)

The Western Front 1917–1918

Peter Simkins

OSPREY
PUBLISHING

First published in Great Britain in 2002 by Osprey Publishing,
Elms Court, Chapel Way, Botley, Oxford OX2 9LP, UK
Email: info@ospreypublishing.com

Every attempt has been made by the publisher to secure the
appropriate permissions for material reproduced in this book. If
there has been any oversight we will be happy to rectify the
situation and written submission should be made to the
Publishers.

ISBN 1 84176 348 9

Editor: Rebecca Cullen
Design: Ken Vail Graphic Design, Cambridge, UK
Cartography by The Map Studio
Index by Alison Worthington
Picture research by Image Select International
Origination by Grasmere Digital Imaging, Leeds, UK
Printed and bound in China by L. Rex Printing Company Ltd.

02 03 04 05 06   10 9 8 7 6 5 4 3 2 1

For a complete list of titles available from Osprey Publishing
please contact:

Osprey Direct UK, PO Box 140,
Wellingborough, Northants, NN8 2FA, UK.
Email: info@ospreydirect.co.uk

Osprey Direct USA, c/o MBI Publishing,
PO Box 1, 729 Prospect Ave,
Osceola, WI 54020, USA.
Email: info@ospreydirectusa.com

www.ospreypublishing.com

This book is one of four titles on the First World War in the
Osprey Essential Histories series

Acknowledgments

The author is grateful to Miss Carole Noakes and to the
Trustees of the Imperial War Museum for permission to quote
from material of which they hold the copyright.

Contents

Introduction

Despite the Herculean exertions and sacrifice of the main protagonists at Verdun and on the Somme in 1916, the Western Front in France and Belgium retained essentially the same shape it had possessed since the advent of the trench warfare stalemate two years before. In 1917, for those astute enough to perceive them, there were signs that the military deadlock might be broken in the near future. By the late spring of 1917 the strategic background to the fighting on the Western Front altered significantly with the Russian Revolution and America's entry into the war. Even the form of the Western Front changed as the German Army – its resources severely strained by the attrition battles of 1916 – adopted a fresh system of flexible defence in depth and, between the Aisne and Arras withdrew to a stronger position known as the Hindenburg Line.

On the Allied side, quite apart from events in Russia and the United States, the balance of military power and effort shifted at an accelerating rate as 1917 wore on. When the breakthrough so confidently predicted by its Commander-in-Chief, Nivelle, failed to materialise from its spring offensive, the exhausted and disillusioned French Army was assailed from within by a wave of mutinies which, for months to come, rendered it largely ineffective as an attacking force. From now onwards, a much bigger share of responsibility for Allied offensive operations on the Western Front fell to the British and Dominion forces under Field-Marshal Sir Douglas Haig. For so long the junior military partners, Haig and the British Expeditionary Force (BEF) correspondingly gained a more influential voice and role in Allied political, strategic and tactical decision-making during the rest of the war.

The BEF had admittedly lost that spirit of breezy optimism with which so many of its citizen-soldiers had been imbued on the eve of the Somme in 1916 but it had simultaneously, if painfully, accrued considerable and invaluable combat experience and was already deeply involved in the tactical and technological learning process that was to transform it into a major player in the ultimate Allied victory in 1918. The BEF's revised fighting methods were, indeed, sufficiently well-honed to enable it to achieve outstanding tactical successes at Vimy Ridge, Messines Ridge and, initially, at Cambrai in 1917. However, the ringing of church bells in Britain to celebrate an apparent victory at Cambrai that November proved premature. The Germans had, by then, developed new artillery and infantry tactics which not only quickly won back most of the ground the British had taken in their final offensive of 1917 but also similarly indicated how mobility would be restored to the Western Front the following year.

For the vast majority of civilians and front-line soldiers on both sides, 1917 nevertheless appeared to offer little promise of victory, becoming a year in which their endurance was tested to the limit. The unrestricted U-boat campaign and the Allied naval blockade respectively increased the prospect of starvation at home in Britain and Germany, while in Canada and Australia debates about the need to introduce conscription revealed some worrying divisions in society and public attitudes to the war. On the Western Front, the bright hopes raised by the early British advances in the Arras and Flanders operations soon dissolved as both battles sank back into the all too familiar pattern of bloody attrition. 1917 is still more often remembered for the mud and casualties of Passchendaele rather than for a story of continuing tactical improvement.

By the same token, Allied and German generals alike – particularly the senior commanders of the BEF – are firmly lodged in the collective folk-memory as 'butchers and bunglers', not as men who learned, relatively swiftly, how to break the trench deadlock by using, more imaginatively, the very weapons that had produced the stalemate in the first place. Curiously, 1918 remains one of the least-known years of the Great War. Depressingly few British citizens today, for example, can identify *any* of the 11 major attacks launched by the BEF between August and November 1918 which together represent the greatest succession of victories in British military history. The London-born Australian historian Eric Andrews has shrewdly remarked: 'Some people seem to assume that to accept that the war ended successfully is to belittle the horror, destruction, suffering and loss of life caused by it.'

In the first of the two volumes dealing with the Western Front, it was pointed out that there was no real alternative to the struggle in France and Belgium. While the bulk of the German Army chose to hold on to its conquests in those two countries, it had to be tackled and beaten there and, as 1918 clearly demonstrated, it was Germany that shored up her allies, not the reverse. This, the second volume, focuses first on the big battles of attrition at Arras, on the Aisne and at Ypres in 1917 and then relates the story of the five offensives initiated by Germany in the spring and summer of 1918 as she strove to achieve victory or a favourable peace before American manpower tipped the scales irrevocably against the Central Powers. Above all, this volume seeks to explain how the BEF survived manpower problems, reorganisation and defensive crises in the first half of 1918 to play a central part, under Foch's direction, in the victorious Allied offensive during the final 100 days of the war.

Chronology

1917 **1 February** Germany begins unrestricted submarine warfare
18–22 February German forces commence preliminary withdrawal from Ancre sector.
12 March Russian Revolution begins.
16 March Germans begin main withdrawal to the Hindenburg Line.
6 April United States of America declares war on Germany.
9 April Opening of British Arras offensive. Canadians storm Vimy Ridge.
16 April French spring offensive begins on the Aisne.
15 May Pétain succeeds Nivelle as French Commander-in-Chief.
7 June British attack Messines Ridge.
31 July Third Battle of Ypres begins.
6 November Passchendaele captured by Canadians.
7 November Bolsheviks seize power in Russia.
16 November Clemenceau becomes French Prime Minister.
20 November Battle of Cambrai begins.
9 December British forces capture Jerusalem.

1918 **3 March**: Peace treaty signed between Russia and the Central Powers at Brest-Litovsk.
21 March: German *Michael* offensive begins in Picardy.
26 March: Foch appointed to co-ordinate Allied operations on Western Front.
9 April: German *Georgette* offensive begins in Flanders.
27 May: German *Blücher* offensive begins on the Aisne.
9 June: Start of German *Gneisenau* offensive.
15 July Last German offensive begins near Reims.
18 July Allied counterstroke on the Marne.
8 August Battle of Amiens begins.
26 September Start of Franco-American offensive in Meuse-Argonne sector.
28 September Start of Allied offensive in Flanders.
29 September British, Australian and American troops open main assault on the Hindenburg Line.
30 September Bulgaria signs armistice.
26 October General Ludendorff resigns.
30 October Turkey signs armistice with the Allies.
3 November Austria-Hungary concludes armistice with the Allies.
9 November Kaiser Wilhelm II abdicates.
11 November Armistice between Allies and Germany ends hostilities on the Western Front.

1919 **28 June** Treaty of Versailles signed.

Strategic choices for 1917

On 15 and 16 October 1916, as the Somme offensive neared its end, Allied military and political leaders met at Chantilly and in Paris to discuss plans for 1917. It was confirmed at these conferences that the Western Front would again be the main theatre of Allied operations in the coming year. Joffre, still the French Commander-in-Chief, had already agreed with Haig, his British counterpart, that the next Franco–British offensive would take the form of a simultaneous assault on a broad frontage, with the French attacking

between the Oise and the Somme while the BEF struck in the sector between Bapaume and Vimy Ridge. Subsidiary attacks would be made on the Aisne and in Upper Alsace. It was also decided, somewhat optimistically, that, should conditions permit, the joint offensive would be launched on or around 1 February. Backed by the War Committee at home, Haig subsequently persuaded Joffre to incorporate his long-desired Flanders offensive in the overall Allied plans for 1917. This latter operation would commence after

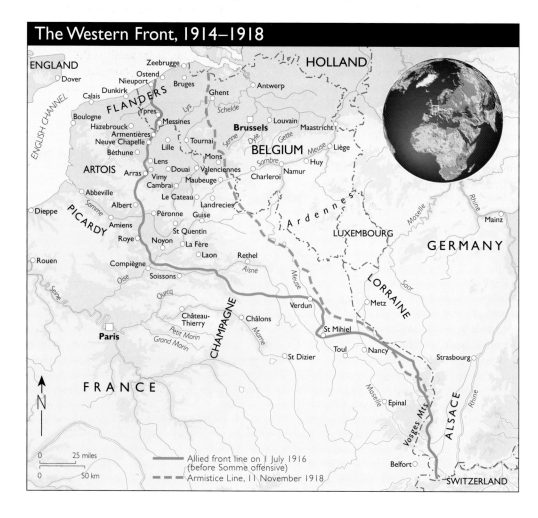

The Western Front, 1914–1918

Allied front line on 1 July 1916 (before Somme offensive)

Armistice Line, 11 November 1918

0   25 miles
0   50 km

the other attacks, probably in the summer, and would involve an advance from the Ypres Salient to clear the whole Belgian coast and capture the German-held ports at Ostend and Zeebrugge.

These plans did not long survive changes of political and military leadership in Britain and France. On 7 December 1916, David Lloyd George, the British Secretary of State for War, succeeded the discredited Asquith as Prime Minster, quickly establishing a more streamlined War Cabinet to ensure a more vigorous prosecution of Britain's war effort. Appalled by the huge casualties on the Somme and anxious to explore strategic options beyond the Western Front, Lloyd George was critical of Haig and of the Chief of the Imperial General Staff, Sir William Robertson, but, because his own political power base remained insecure, he stopped short of actually removing them. Nevertheless, events on the *other* side of the Channel presented him with an early chance to erode their individual and combined authority.

Joffre, the hero of the Marne, had come under increasing censure in the French Chamber of Deputies for Allied losses and setbacks in 1916 – especially those at Verdun. To deflect criticism away from his government, the French Prime Minister, Aristide Briand, induced Joffre to retire, sugaring the bitter pill by creating him a Marshal. On 12 December Joffre was replaced as Commander-in-Chief by General Robert Nivelle, the architect of the later successes at Verdun. An articulate and immensely self-confident gunner with an English mother, Nivelle was convinced that his recent artillery tactics, if applied on a much bigger scale, would at last bring the Allies genuine victory on the Western Front. He believed that a massive saturation bombardment, followed by a creeping barrage of great depth and by furious infantry attacks, would suffice to pierce the enemy's front defences and help his troops

to reach the German gun line in a single bound. A decisive 'rupture' or breakthrough would then surely follow within two days.

In Nivelle's proposed alterations to the Allied plan, it was envisaged that British and French forces would carry out preliminary attacks between Arras and the Oise to pin down German reserves. The principal blow would now be delivered by the French on the Aisne, where a 'mass of manoeuvre' comprising some 27 divisions would be kept in readiness to exploit the expected rupture of the German front. Haig, who was himself promoted to Field-Marshal on 27 December 1916, at first found Nivelle 'straightforward and soldierly' and, though he had some reservations, initially supported the new scheme in general terms. The BEF had been assigned only a subsidiary role in the modified offensive, yet, to release French formations for Nivelle's 'mass of manoeuvre', was being asked to take over an additional 20 miles of front, as far south as the Amiens–Roye area. Haig, however, was primarily concerned with his cherished Flanders plan and was prepared to

General Robert Nivelle, the French Commander-in-Chief from December 1916 to May 1917.
(Ann Ronan Picture library)

David Lloyd George, British Prime Minister from
December 1916 until 1922. (IWM)

co-operate in Nivelle's grand scheme as
long as the projected operations in Belgium
were not compromised.

Eager to seek any plausible alternative to
more long months of attrition, the Allied
political leaders were all too willing to be
swayed by Nivelle's seductive proposals. For

instance, Lloyd George – while willing to
shift the emphasis of British strategy and
reinforce peripheral war zones – nevertheless
accepted that the German Army must be
defeated on the Western Front and was
therefore content to approve Nivelle's ideas.
If the new French plan was successful, Lloyd
George could bask in reflected glory but, if it
failed, his own case for an alternative
strategic approach would be greatly

enhanced. Certainly Lloyd George soon glimpsed an opportunity to turn Nivelle's increasing irritation with Haig to his own account and thereby weaken the influence of his generals. When a conference was convened at Calais on 26–27 February, ostensibly to discuss the need to improve the overburdened railway communications behind the British zone of operations, it rapidly became evident that Lloyd George had conspired with the French – behind the backs of Robertson and Haig – in an attempt to make the British Commander-in-Chief permanently subordinate to Nivelle. This would deprive Haig of a role in the preparation of Allied plans and leave him with nothing much more than responsibility for the BEF's discipline and personnel. An outraged Robertson threatened to resign and Lloyd George, faced with further pressure from King George V and the War Cabinet, chose to avoid a full-blown political crisis by watering down the Calais proposals. The BEF would keep its distinct identity and Haig would be subordinate to the French Commander-in-Chief only for the duration of the coming offensive. The incident, however, did little to encourage closer co-operation between the British and French armies or boost the prospects of a unified Allied command. It also deepened the underlying antipathy between Lloyd George and his senior commanders on the Western Front.

Germany similarly witnessed growing disagreements among her military and political leaders in the opening weeks of 1917. Theobald von Bethmann-Hollweg, the German Chancellor, favoured a negotiated peace settlement, while Hindenburg, the Chief of the General Staff, and Ludendorff – his 'First Quartermaster-General' and *de facto* controller of Germany's war effort – were still totally committed to outright victory. At the insistence of the High Command, the so-called 'Hindenburg Programme', designed to increase munitions production, and an

Auxiliary Service Law, to mobilise the nation's human resources more systematically, had both been adopted in the last quarter of 1916. Germany was unwilling to abandon her main war aims which, at this point, included holding on to Liège and the maintenance of military, economic and political influence over Belgium – her reluctance to compromise having contributed to the failure of the recent peace feelers put out by both sides.

As in Britain and France, public opinion in Germany in early 1917 would have undoubtedly viewed anything less than a clear-cut victory as a betrayal of all who had shed their blood in the national cause. Germany's immediate future, however, looked far from bright. The Allied blockade was already causing disturbing shortages and hardship on the home front and Ludendorff recognised that Allied superiority in *matériel* and manpower made it unlikely that Germany could win a decisive success on land in 1917. In his mind, the surest path to victory would be to hasten Britain's collapse by ordering a resumption of unrestricted submarine warfare against Allied and neutral shipping. Such a policy carried obvious risks. The United States, angered by previous U-boat campaigns in 1915 and 1916, might this time throw in her lot with the Allies and enter the war against the Central Powers. Ludendorff, however, judged that the U-boats would achieve the necessary result before America could fully deploy her considerable military and industrial potential against Germany.

In the end Ludendorff's arguments held sway. It was decreed by the Kaiser that unrestricted submarine operations should begin on 1 February. Germany, meanwhile, would remain on the defensive on the Western Front for the foreseeable future. As Ludendorff's star approached its zenith, Bethmann-Hollweg's influence waned and he resigned, some six months later, on 13 July.

The opposing armies

At the time of the conference at Chantilly in mid-November 1916, the Allies outnumbered the Germans in infantry divisions on the Western Front, with 169 divisions against 129. Of the Allied divisions, 107 were French, 56 were British and six were Belgian. Despite having suffered terrible losses on the Somme, the BEF, however, continued to expand in the following months. Although the 60th Division was then preparing to move to Salonika, six more British Territorial divisions were to cross to France by the end of February 1917 while a fifth Australian division reached the Western Front in late November 1916, bringing the number of Dominion divisions in the BEF to 10 – five from Australia, four from Canada and one from New Zealand. The overall strength of the BEF rose from just over 1,500,000 in November 1916 to a peak of 2,044,627 on 1 August 1917.

Crucially, the BEF also received increasing numbers of heavy guns and howitzers. In July 1916 it had possessed 761 such weapons. By November that year this total had risen to 1,157 and it was estimated that the latter figure would more than double by April 1917. The supply of heavy artillery ammunition similarly grew from 706,222 rounds in the second quarter of 1916 to over 5,000,000 in the corresponding period of 1917. Stocks of field gun ammunition rose almost to the same extent, 50 Mark II tanks were to supplement the 70 older Mark I tanks in January 1917 and the improved Mark IV model would be delivered later in the year.

During the winter of 1916–1917 the BEF made strenuous efforts to disseminate the lessons it had learned on the Somme and to make appropriate improvements in its fighting methods, particularly in its artillery and small-unit infantry tactics. These months were notable for the publication of two

important manuals. December 1916 saw the issue of *Instructions for the Training of Divisions for Offensive Action*, which helped to lay the foundations of the co-ordinated all-arms tactics that would prove so effective in the final months of the war. This was followed, in February 1917, by the no less influential *Instructions for the Training of Platoons for Offensive Action*, which heralded a major change in the emphasis of infantry tactics from the company to the smaller sub-unit of the platoon. In 1915–1916 the company, composed principally of riflemen, constituted the basic tactical unit, with the specialists – such as machine-gunners, snipers and bombers (grenade-throwers)- forming *separate* sections. In 1917 the platoon (of which there were four in each company) was itself organised into four specialist fighting sections. One contained the riflemen, including a sniper and a scout; another contained the bombers; a third was built around rifle grenades – 'the infantry's howitzer'; and the fourth was a Lewis light machine-gun section. In other words, the infantry company now comprised four flexible platoon *teams*, each capable of waging its own battle in miniature, using a variety of modern weapons. It would be some time before the full impact of these changes was felt, but there would be clear, if not yet universal, signs of improvement in the BEF's infantry tactics in 1917.

The French Army would be able to deploy 110 divisions on the Western Front by 1 April 1917 but this slight increase was more apparent than real, for there was no rise in the number of infantry battalions available. Nevertheless, the French artillery arm was still growing, with 4,970 heavy guns and howitzers expected to be available by the spring – an increase of nearly 700 pieces over the November 1916 total. In addition, the production of tanks was now in hand

and the St Chamond and Schneider models would play a part in the Allied spring offensive of 1917. The French had likewise profited from the tactical lessons of 1916 but both the fighting capacity and morale of the French Army were unquestionably more brittle after the ordeal of Verdun.

The first elements of two Portuguese divisions began to arrive in France early in January 1917 and were subsequently attached to the BEF. The six large Belgian divisions were not all they seemed. Not only had Belgium deliberately adopted a defensive strategy since the end of 1914 but also, until the autumn of 1918, the standards of training and equipment and the strength of her reserves would simply not allow her forces to do more than hold quiet sectors.

The condition of the German Army at the end of 1916 was causing its commanders and senior staff officers great anxiety. For example, the German divisions which were involved in the December operations at Verdun only had a combat strength of between 3,000 and 6,000 rifles and were forced to deploy some two-thirds of their troops in the front line. About 60 per cent of the German divisions on the Western Front in 1916 had also been through the mincing-machine of the Somme, a battlefield which one staff officer described as 'the muddy grave of the German field army'. It did not help matters that much of the pain the Germans had suffered on the Somme had been inflicted by the relatively inexperienced citizen-soldiers and staffs of the expanding BEF. Von Kuhl, the distinguished Chief of Staff to Crown Prince Rupprecht of Bavaria's Army Group, warned on 17 January 1917 that 'we can no longer reckon on the old troops; there is no doubt

that in the past summer and autumn our troops have been fearfully harried and wasted'. Rest and training, he advised, must come 'first and foremost' in 1917. Although the Germans decided to create more than a dozen new divisions, this could only be done by reducing existing establishments or drawing upon reserves. The increase therefore represented an organisational or administrative adjustment rather than a real reinforcement.

When 1917 began most of the German divisions in France and Belgium formed part of two Army Groups. The Army Group commanded by Crown Prince Wilhelm, the Kaiser's son and heir to the Imperial throne, held the line from the Swiss frontier to a point north of Reims and included the Third and Fifth Armies as well as the three smaller Army Detachments A, B and C. The 170-mile stretch from north of Reims to the River Lys was the responsibility of Crown Prince Rupprecht of Bavaria's Army Group, which comprised the First, Sixth and Seventh Armies. The sector from the Lys to the coast came under an independent Fourth Army, commanded by Duke Albrecht of Württemberg. In March 1917 changes were made in these arrangements. The Fourth Army, now commanded by General Sixt von Arnim, was incorporated into Crown Prince Rupprecht's Army Group; the three Army Detachments on the German left were linked together to form a third Army Group under Duke Albrecht; and the Seventh Army was transferred from Crown Prince Rupprecht's Army Group to that of Crown Prince Wilhelm so that all the formations likely to be facing the expected French offensive in the spring would all be under one command.

War on the Western Front, 1917–1918

Alberich: The Germans withdraw

Germany's decision to remain on the defensive in the west was made easier by the strides made in the construction of the fresh positions which were being established 25 miles to the rear of the existing front and which incorporated all the basic principles of the new doctrine of flexible defence in depth. The key stretch, built since September 1916, extended from Neuville Vitasse, near Arras, through St Quentin and Laffaux to Cerny, east of Soissons. The system – named the *Siegfried Stellung* by the Germans but called the Hindenburg Line by the British – was essentially a series of defensive zones rather than a single line. Any force approaching it would first face an outpost zone, around 600 yards deep, which contained concrete dug-outs sheltering small detachments of storm troops. The latter were deployed to mount instant counter-attacks and check the momentum of an Allied advance. Behind the outpost zone was a main 'battle zone' which ran back some 2,500 yards and included the first and second trench lines as well as many concrete machine-gun posts with interlocking fields of fire. Counter-attack divisions were placed immediately to the rear of the battle zone. Subsequently two more zones were added, giving the system a depth of up to 8,000 yards. The trench lines were protected by thick belts of barbed wire, laid out in a zig-zag pattern nearest the front trench so that machine-guns could cover the angles of exit. The Germans also built the *Wotan Stellung*, a northern branch of the

German barbed wire defences on the Hindenburg Line. (IWM)

Hindenburg Line, between Drocourt and Quéant, near Arras.

From a military standpoint, withdrawal to the Hindenburg Line made sense for the Germans but even Ludendorff wavered, fearing that retirement might adversely affect the morale of German soldiers and civilians. The move was forced upon him by Crown Prince Rupprecht of Bavaria, the Army Group commander in whose sector the Hindenburg Line was largely located. Already under renewed pressure from the British Fifth Army on the Ancre, Rupprecht and his outstanding Chief-of-Staff, von Kuhl, informed Ludendorff that the present positions were poor and that the troops were in no state to endure a repeat of the 1916 Somme battle. The order for the retirement was accordingly issued on 4 February 1917.

The scheme for the rearward movement was code-named *Alberich*, after the malicious dwarf of the *Niebelung* Saga. This was appropriate since the withdrawal was accompanied by a 'scorched earth' policy. Rupprecht was appalled by the scale and

methods of the proposed destruction and was only narrowly dissuaded from resigning when it was observed that this might appear to signal a rift between Bavaria and the rest of Germany. Despite his objections, the *Alberich* programme began on 9 February. Throughout the area being abandoned, the Germans felled trees, blew up railways and roads, polluted wells, razed towns and villages to the ground and planted countless mines and booby-traps. While children, mothers and the elderly were left behind with minimal rations, over 125,000 able-bodied French civilians were transported to work elsewhere in the German-occupied zone.

The main phase of the retirement commenced on 16 March and was largely completed within four days. The evacuation of the Noyon salient, and the withdrawal from the smaller salient near Bapaume, shortened the German front by 25 miles, freed 14 divisions and seriously disrupted

A railway station and sidings are blown up by the retreating Germans, 1 April 1917. (IWM)

Gottstrafe England

Allied plans for the spring. It was not easy for the Allies to advance rapidly across a devastated region after the most severe winter of the war but it can equally be argued that the pursuit of the Germans was too cautious. The preparations for the French Northern Army Group's subsidiary part in the spring offensive were, in fact, well in hand and, on 4 March, General Franchet d'Esperey, its commander, had sought permission to attack vigorously as soon as possible in order to catch the Germans at a critical moment. Nivelle, however, would not countenance major revisions to his own operational plan and refused to sanction anything other than a limited assault to capture the German front position. Thus he missed his only real opportunity to upset the German withdrawal.

Curtain-raiser at Arras

Since Nivelle refused to modify his strategy, the BEF's contribution to the spring offensive – an attack on a 14-mile front at Arras – was still primarily intended to lure German

British soldiers with French children in the newly -liberated village of Vraignes, 20 March 1917. (IWM)

reserves away from the main French effort on the Aisne. The British Third Army, commanded by General Sir Edmund Allenby, would strike east of Arras, attempting to penetrate the Hindenburg Line on its right and the older German defence lines opposite its centre and left. Allenby's units would then try to take the Hindenburg position from the rear and flank as well as moving on Cambrai. Vimy Ridge, to Allenby's north, would be assaulted by the Canadian Corps, part of General Sir Henry Horne's First Army. Forty-eight tanks and more than 2,800 guns would support the initial operations.

The German withdrawal had most severely dislocated the British plan on Allenby's southern flank, in the sector of General Sir Hubert Gough's Fifth Army. One of Gough's original objectives, the Bapaume salient, had vanished and the Fifth Army experienced considerable problems in hauling its artillery across the devastated zone. Consequently, the only assistance

The German withdrawal, February–April 1917

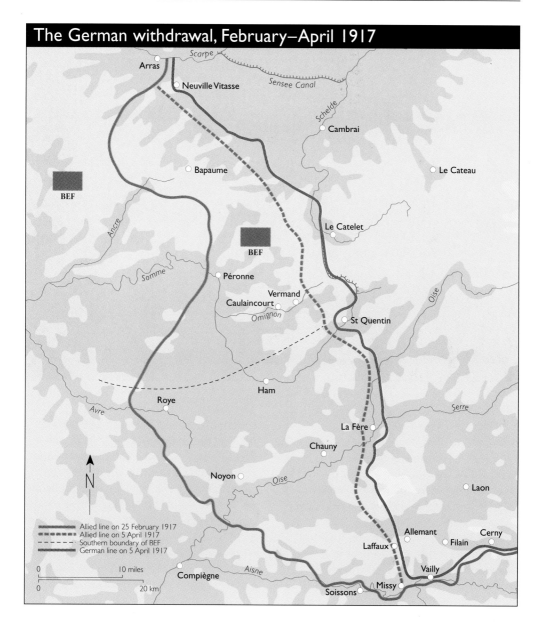

Arras
Scarpe
Neuville Vitasse
Sensee Canal
Schelde
Cambrai
Bapaume
Le Cateau
BEF
Ancre
Le Catelet
BEF
Somme
Péronne
Vermand
Caulaincourt
Omignon
St Quentin
Oise
Ham
Roye
Serre
Avre
La Fère
Chauny
Noyon
Oise
Laon
Allied line on 25 February 1917
Allied line on 5 April 1917
Southern boundary of BEF
German line on 5 April 1917
Allemant
Cerny
Laffaux
Filain
0   10 miles
Vailly
0   20 km
Compiègne
Aisne
Missy
Soissons
N

Gough could offer Allenby was to attack the Hindenburg Line on a relatively narrow front at Bullecourt, close to its junction with the Drocourt–Quéant Line (*Wotan Stellung*). The major assault by the First and Third Armies was scheduled for 8 April while the more limited attack by the Fifth Army would be delivered a day or so later.

The French Northern Army Group's projected attack between the Somme and the Oise was similarly neutralised by the German retirement and was scaled down to a minor

operation at St Quentin. This meant that, on a 60-mile length of front between Bullecourt and the Aisne, the Germans faced negligible pressure. The operations at Vimy and Arras therefore assumed even greater significance as a means of pinning down German reserve formations.

The opening stages of the Battle of Arras would reveal the extent to which the BEF had acted upon the painful tactical lessons of the Somme offensive of 1916. Major-General Holland, Allenby's artillery

Lieutenant-General the Hon. Sir Julian Byng, who commanded the Canadian Corps and later the British Third Army in 1917. (IWM)

commander, advocated a preliminary bombardment lasting only 48 hours but Haig and his own artillery adviser, Major-General Birch, opted instead for a four-day bombardment, wishing to ensure that the defenders were subjected to the maximum strain and that the German wire was properly cut. Haig and Birch also rightly judged that British artillery techniques and training were still not quite up to the tasks which Allenby and Holland proposed to set the gunners. The views of Haig and Birch prevailed and, in the event, the four-day bombardment was extended by 24 hours, partly as a result of bad weather but also at the request of the French. Forty tanks were available to support the Third Army yet were allotted to three different corps in groups of 16 or less.

If the lengthy bombardment and the deployment of tanks in 'penny packets' were reminders of the Somme, the planning for

Arras nevertheless showed evidence of considerable improvements in various areas, not least the artillery. The ratio of one gun to every 10–12 yards of front in the Arras assault compared favourably with the one gun per 20 yards of July 1916; ammunition was more reliable and supplies more abundant; the introduction of the instantaneous '106' fuze – albeit in small quantities – afforded a more efficient means of cutting enemy barbed wire without cratering the ground; much greater emphasis was placed upon precise target selection rather than indiscriminate general bombardments; and marked progress had been made in the BEF's ability to locate enemy batteries by sound-ranging and flash-spotting. Overhead machine-gun barrages to assist advancing infantry were now a standard ingredient of British offensive operations. Furthermore, through methodical and imaginative staff work, the extensive system of cellars, caves and sewers under Arras was exploited and developed to provide secure shelters for attacking troops, guaranteeing that they would be fresher for the assault. Six miles of subways – most of which were lit by

electricity – were excavated for the same reason in the chalk under Vimy Ridge.

Scaling ladders being erected in a British trench on 8 April 1917, the eve of the assault at Arras. (IWM)

Arras: Early successes

All this planning and preparation produced impressive initial results when the BEF's assault at Arras was launched in snow and sleet on Easter Monday, 9 April 1917. On the potentially troublesome right flank of the Third Army, VII Corps captured the strongly -fortified village of Neuville Vitasse and won some footholds in the Hindenburg Line's front trenches. In the centre – especially north of Telegraph Hill, where the Hindenburg Line ended – VI Corps pushed forward between two and three miles. Just south of the River Scarpe, battalions of the 15th (Scottish) and 12th (Eastern) Divisions charged down the eastern side of Observation Ridge to seize 67 German field guns which had been deployed in the open along Battery Valley. Even more dramatic gains were achieved by the troops of XVII Corps, whose thrust of three-and-a-half

miles to Fampoux represented the longest advance made in one day by any army on the Western Front since the trench deadlock imposed itself in late 1914.

The encouraging early gains made by the Third Army were more than matched by the assault on the greatly-prized Vimy Ridge by the Canadian Corps under Lieutenant-General Sir Julian Byng. Although the 1st and 2nd Canadian Divisions on the right had to advance up to 4,000 yards, they soon secured their principal objectives around Thélus and Farbus, The 3rd Canadian Division, in the centre, took La Folie Farm and the western edge of La Folie Wood but ran into difficulties on its left flank, where the 4th Canadian Division was unable to secure the summit of Hill 145 – the highest point on the ridge – until the evening. On the extreme left, Hill 120 ('The Pimple') stayed in German possession for another three days, falling to an attack by the 4th Canadian Division before daybreak on

Arras: The infantry assault plan, 9 April 1917

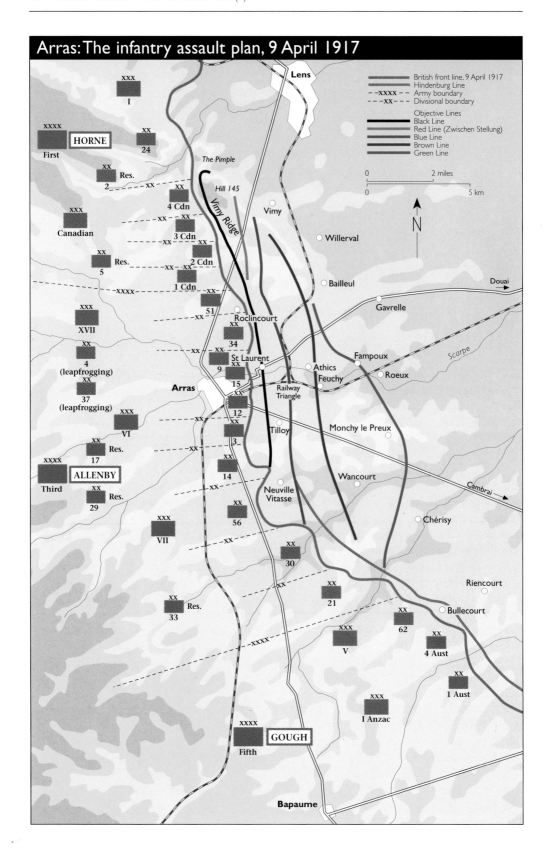

Germans surrender as Canadian support waves cross Vimy Ridge, 9 April 1917. (IWM)

12 April. By then the Canadians had consolidated their new positions along the crest of the main ridge. The storming of Vimy Ridge, one of the truly outstanding operations of the war, had seen the four Canadian divisions attacking simultaneously for the first time. Their success, accomplished at a cost of 11,297 casualties, not only gave a huge boost to Canada's growing sense of nationhood but also provided the BEF with a physical bulwark which would prove of immense value in the defensive battles of 1918.

Meanwhile, up to 11 April, Allenby's Third Army had seized 112 guns and 7,000 prisoners, incurring only 8,238 casualties in the process. The relatively inexpensive early progress of the First and Third Armies at Arras contrasted sharply with the disasters of the opening day of the 1916 Somme offensive. However, success was more elusive on the Fifth Army's front at Bullecourt. Here Gough rashly endorsed a last-minute suggestion from a junior officer

that a dozen tanks should breach the German wire for the infantry in a surprise attack, without any previous rehearsals or supporting barrage. Following a false start on 10 April, Gough again displayed poor judgement by allowing this ill-prepared venture to proceed, essentially unchanged, the next day. All but four of the tanks failed to appear at the start line on time and most were eventually hit or broke down, leaving the attacking brigades of the 4th Australian Division to advance against the largely uncut wire of the Hindenburg Line with no accompanying barrage. Remarkably, these splendid troops reached and entered the second line of German trenches but were denied direct artillery support because of highly misleading reports about the headway made by the tanks and equally false information that men of the British 62nd Division had been spotted in Bullecourt village. The surviving Australians were forced to withdraw by early afternoon, the 4th Australian Brigade alone having suffered 2,339 casualties out of 3,000 who went into action. A total of 1,182 officers and men of I Anzac Corps were captured, the

British infantry, 18-pounder guns and a tank near Feuchy crossroads, Arras, April 1917. (IWM)

total number of Australian prisoners in a single action during the Great War. The whole sorry episode simply served to increase Australian distrust both of tanks and of British generalship.

The Germans also committed mistakes which added to their own difficulties in the opening phases of the battle. The commander of the German Sixth Army at Arras, Colonel-General von Falkenhausen, failed to apply some key principles of the new system of defence in depth. Too many infantrymen were placed in the forward zone and his counter-attack divisions were kept so far back that they were between 12 and 24 hours' march from the battlefield. The expert tactician Colonel von Lossberg – whose nickname was 'the fireman of the Western Front' – was brought in as Chief of Staff of the Sixth Army and speedily reorganised the defence.

The dominating village of Monchy le Preux, perched on high ground in the centre of the battlefield, was captured on 11 April by the British 37th Division and units of the 15th (Scottish) Division and 3rd Cavalry Division, although VI Corps was unable to make immediate progress eastwards, beyond Monchy, to Infantry Hill. As German reserves closed gaps in the line, the British advance lost momentum. The problems of communicating on the battlefield and of moving artillery forward across broken ground quickly enough to deal with German rear positions remained largely insoluble, and British junior officers and other ranks did not yet possess the tactical skill to adapt to semi-open warfare once the initial assault had breached the enemy line. The growing German resistance was reflected in the change in tone in Allenby's orders to the British Third Army. On 11 April he stressed that 'risks must be freely taken' in pursuing 'a defeated enemy'. The following day he merely directed that pressure on the Germans must be maintained to prevent them from consolidating their positions. However, the imminence of the Nivelle offensive made it impossible for Haig and Allenby to shut down the Arras operations at this point.

Dashed hopes: The Nivelle offensive

Haig was hardly encouraged by the fact that Nivelle's preparations had been plagued by problems. On 20 March Aristide Briand's government fell and the new French Prime Minister, Alexandre Ribot, entrusted the Ministry of War to Paul Painlevé, a Socialist with little faith in Nivelle's ideas. At the same time the German withdrawal to the Hindenburg Line largely nullified the French Northern Army Group's planned contribution to the offensive. The German retirement did have some benefits for the French since it enabled the Northern Army Group to release 13 divisions and 550 heavy artillery pieces for use elsewhere. It also gave the French the opportunity to assault the flank of the German position north of the Aisne and to direct enfilade artillery fire against the western portion of the defences on the Chemin des Dames ridge.

Pétain urged that the extra units now available should be transferred to his Central Army Group so that he could undertake a major attack astride the Suippe east of Reims – an operation that would create considerable difficulties for the Germans and more than compensate for the enforced reduction in scope of the Northern Army Group's effort. The chief drawback to Pétain's proposals was that the Central Army Group would not be ready to attack before 1 May and Nivelle felt that he could not risk postponing the principal offensive for a further two weeks. He therefore decided to restrict the Central Army Group's role to an attack by its left wing on the Moronvilliers heights, between Reims and the Suippe. Most of the reserves were allocated, in principle, to the newly-created Reserve Army Group, commanded by General Micheler, but were initially kept under Nivelle's own control.

To add to Nivelle's troubles, Micheler – whose Army Group was expected to achieve and exploit the breakthrough on the Aisne – had serious misgivings about the coming offensive. In a letter to Nivelle on 22 March, Micheler pointed out that the Germans too had extra reserves available as a result of their withdrawal to the Hindenburg Line. Moreover, he observed that, since Nivelle's plan was originally conceived, the Germans had strengthened and deepened their defences in the key sector, increasing the number of successive defensive positions there from two to four. Consequently it might no longer prove possible for the Reserve Army Group to effect a breakthrough as quickly as Nivelle required.

Although Micheler's anxieties were shared by the other Army Group commanders, Nivelle would not make any fundamental amendments to his overall plan or chosen tactics. With the help of Colonel Messimy, a Deputy and former Minister of War, Micheler therefore made his views known to the Prime Minister. On 6 April, the very day that the United States declared war on Germany, a Council of War took place, in President Poincaré's presence, at Compiègne. Painlevé, who emphasised that the Russian Revolution in March ruled out any relief from that quarter, felt that the offensive should be postponed until the Americans could participate. Micheler and Pétain again expressed doubts that the attacking troops could penetrate the defences beyond the German second position and argued for a more limited operation. President Poincaré, summing up, proposed that the offensive should proceed but should be halted if it failed to rupture the German front. At this juncture, Nivelle decided to call the bluff of his critics by offering to resign. The assembled politicians, clearly unwilling to push matters that far, hastened to reassure Nivelle that they had complete confidence in him and the meeting ended with the main issues left unresolved. All that the protests had achieved was to impose greater pressure on the Commander-in-Chief. The following day he received more unpalatable news. During an attack south of the Aisne on 4 April, the Germans had apparently captured plans of the French assault. Even so, Nivelle obstinately refused to adapt his scheme to meet the changed circumstances.

Supported by 3,810 guns, the French Fifth and Sixth Armies began the offensive

The Nivelle offensive: Opening phase

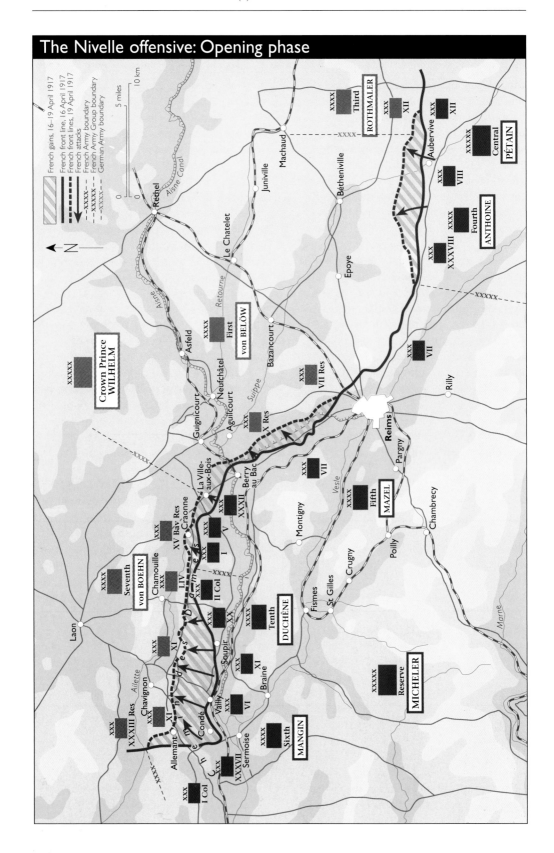

along a 25-mile front on 16 April, a week after the British assault at Arras. Their spirits lifted by Nivelle's stirring pronouncements, the French troops went into action with much of their customary *élan*. However, because the new German defensive doctrine dictated that the forward positions should be lightly held, the effects of the 14-day preliminary bombardment were greatly reduced and the French had deployed too few howitzers to reach into all the quarries, caves and ravines which dotted this sector. Hence the French captured the German first line in many places merely to find themselves facing massed machine-guns in a comparatively untouched German second position. Even the use of 128 tanks by Mazel's Fifth Army did not produce the desired breakthrough. The only gains – a three-mile advance near Juvincourt – were, in fact, less significant than those achieved in the BEF's initial attack at Arras seven days before.

Nivelle attempted, on 17 April, to exploit the Fifth Army's progress in the right centre yet, unexpectedly, the most dramatic successes occurred on the left. Steady pressure there by Mangin's Sixth Army obliged the Germans to pull back around four miles, abandoning the Laffaux-Condé-Braye area as well as huge stocks of ammunition and numerous undamaged guns. In Champagne, the Central Army Group also opened its subsidiary offensive on 17 April and its Fourth Army, commanded by General Anthoine, took several important heights over the next four days. In all, by 20 April, the French Fourth, Fifth and Sixth Armies had seized over 20,000 prisoners and 147 guns. These were impressive results by the standards of previous years but there was no decisive breakthrough on the Aisne. The vast expenditure of shells by the French soon led to a worrying shell shortage and, by 25 April, French casualties totalled 96,125. The French medical services broke down under the strain and the growing delays in evacuating wounded from the forward zone further demoralised front-line troops.

Nivelle's personal influence on events began to diminish before the French offensive

A French St Chamond tank at Condé-sur-Aisne, 3 May 1917. (IWM)

was a week old. On 21 April, Duchêne's Tenth Army was moved up into the line between the Fifth and Sixth Armies but Micheler persuaded Nivelle to scale down the offensive to a more limited operation designed to secure the whole of the Chemin des Dames ridge and drive the Germans away from Reims. Nivelle himself became increasingly depressed as every decision and order was subjected to intense scrutiny by the government and, on 29 April, his authority was further undermined when Pétain was appointed Chief of the General Staff and given powers which, in effect, made him the

government's main military adviser. Mangin was another scapegoat, being removed from command of the Sixth Army on 2 May.

A fresh series of French attacks was undertaken on 4 and 5 May. The Sixth Army, now under General Maistre, thrust deep into the German-held salient opposite Laffaux and took the German positions on a two-and-a-half-mile sector along the Chemin des Dames. Meanwhile, troops of the Tenth Army captured the remainder of the Californie plateau at the eastern extremity of the ridge. These successes were not sufficient to repair Nivelle's crumbling reputation.

Measured against the terrible yardstick of Verdun, the totals of 187,000 French and 163,000 German casualties for the whole offensive were not overwhelmingly high. Nevertheless, because Nivelle had promised so much, the shock of disappointment felt by the French Army and people when the breakthrough failed to materialise was all the more severe. As a wave of unrest and indiscipline engulfed the French Army, Nivelle was dismissed from the post of Commander-in-Chief on 15 May. His place was taken by Pétain, with Foch succeeding the latter as Chief of the French General Staff.

Taking the strain

The faltering start to Nivelle's offensive made it all the more vital for the BEF to continue operations at Arras, if only to deter the Germans from moving additional reserves to the Aisne. Despite his successes between 9 and 11 April, Allenby's subsequent handling of the battle caused the commanders of the 17th, 29th and 50th Divisions to register a formal protest against isolated, narrow-front operations which exposed attacking troops to concentrated flanking fire. On 15 April Allenby learned that Haig had ordered a pause to prepare another large-scale co-ordinated attack.

With all chances of surprise gone, Haig – expecting attrition rather than breakthrough – decided that this time the objectives would be less ambitious than on 9 April. After he had conferred with Allenby, Horne and Gough, it was agreed that nine British and Canadian divisions of the First and Third Armies would deliver the next set-piece blow along a nine-mile front against the line Gavrelle–Roeux–Guémappe–Fontaine lez Croisilles.

When the attack began on 23 April, the BEF realised that, under von Lossberg's direction, the German Sixth Army has at last grasped the principles of flexible zonal defence. A fortnight earlier the German artillery had been overpowered but it was now present in greater strength. Furthermore, German battery positions were less precisely identified than before and many were beyond the range of British heavy guns, rendering the BEF's counter-battery fire much less effective. British and Dominion staff officers were still unaccustomed to improvising once the set-piece assault phase was over so, all too often, increasingly weary divisions were supported only by weak or patchy barrages as they advanced into the teeth of fearsome German artillery and machine-gun fire north

Wounded British prisoners after the 3st Division's attack at Oppy Wood, 3 May 1917. (IWM)

and south of the River Scarpe. The
15th (Scottish) Division pushed the Germans
out of Guémappe and, in the First Army's
sector, the 63rd (Royal Naval) Division
captured Gavrelle, facilitating the seizure,
within two days, of around two miles of
tactically valuable ground near the
Roeux–Gavrelle road. For the infantrymen
involved, however, the fighting of
23–24 April was some of the toughest of the
war, characterised by the bitter see-saw
struggle for the heavily-fortified village of
Roeux and its Chemical Works.

By now Haig had cause for serious concern
about the French offensive. He was prepared
to press on at Arras to prevent the initiative
from passing to the Germans but, as U-boats
exacted a growing toll of Allied and neutral
shipping, the need to reclaim the Belgian
ports became even more important. Aiming

Men of the French 313th Infantry Regiment on the Montigny road in the Marne region, 7 June 1917. (IWM)

3 May were already tired and below strength or contained a large proportion of green conscripts. The Canadian Corps, on the First Army's front, again performed well, seizing Fresnoy, and, in the Fifth Army's sector, Brigadier-General Gellibrand's 6th Australian Brigade won a precarious foothold in the Hindenburg Line close to Bullecourt but elsewhere progress was minimal. Efforts to extend the gains at Bullecourt, led to a savage struggle in which seven British and Australian divisions became enmeshed before the 58th (London) Division finally cleared the village on 17 May. Further north, Roeux and the Chemical Works were at last taken by the British between 11 and 14 May although the Germans had earlier recaptured Fresnoy.

In all, from 9 April to 17 May, the BEF incurred losses of 159,000 at Arras. This total represented the highest daily casualty rate – averaging 4,076 – of any major British offensive in the Great War. For the BEF the battle had degenerated, after the bright promise of 9 April, into yet another slogging-match which consumed not only men but also time which Haig sorely needed to ensure the success of his operations in Flanders. On the other hand, Haig had more than fulfilled his obligations to the French and was released from his subordination to Nivelle when the latter was removed from command in mid-May. Allenby was another command casualty of the offensive. His relations with Haig had never been warm and he had come under mounting criticism for his conduct of the later phases of the Arras offensive. On 6 June Allenby was transferred to Palestine to command the Egyptian Expeditionary Force and was replaced at the head of Third Army by Byng.

Mutinies

The Nivelle offensive was barely under way when, on 17 April, the French Army began to experience its worst *internal* crisis

to divert German attention away from both Flanders and the Aisne, to exhaust enemy reserves and secure a tenable defensive line east of Arras, Haig ordered a third big set-piece attack, which began on 3 May. However, knowing that he must save his own reserves for the forthcoming offensive in Flanders, he chose not to employ fresh divisions at Arras. Consequently, many of the formations participating in the attack of of the war. That day, 17 soldiers of the 108th Infantry Regiment left their posts in the face of the enemy. This was the first in a series of acts of collective indiscipline which, after reaching a peak in June, continued into the autumn. By 23 October some 250 such incidents had occurred, all but 12 in infantry units. Sixty-eight out of 112 French divisions were affected by the wave of mutinies.

The widespread unrest manifested itself in a variety of forms, including peace demands, the singing of revolutionary songs, stone-throwing and the breaking of windows. Far more serious were cases of incendiarism, mass demonstrations and the refusal by substantial numbers of men to return to the front line. Many indicated that while they were ready to hold defensive positions they were no longer willing to participate in apparently futile assaults. However, one should beware of exaggerating the extent of the mutinies or their revolutionary intent. Long-felt grievances about front-line conditions, envy of the relative comfort enjoyed by industrial workers on high wages, and a sudden and spontaneous tide of despondency after the failure of the spring offensive all seem to have played a more fundamental role than political agitation or pacifist subversion in fomenting unrest.

Having succeeded Nivelle as Commander-in-Chief in mid-May, Pétain eventually managed to repair the morale and fighting capacity of the French Army with a combination of reform, understanding and iron discipline. Three thousand, four hundred and twenty-seven French soldiers were convicted by courts-martial for offences arising from the mutinies. Of these, 554 were sentenced to death and 49 (or eight per cent) were actually executed. At the same time, Pétain renounced the concept of the offensive at all costs, ruling out further large-scale attacks until the United States Army reached France in strength and weapons production had considerably increased. 'I am waiting for the Americans and the tanks', Pétain frequently declared. He also took rapid action to address the most

common complaints of front-line soldiers, improving medical services, welfare facilities, accommodation and food as well as granting additional leave. The French Army recovered sufficiently by late August to deliver a well-planned assault at Verdun which led to the recapture of the heights of the *Mort Homme* and *Côte 304*. Another attack, at Malmaison in October, saw the French win possession of the crest of the Chemin des Dames ridge on the Aisne. Nevertheless these were limited affairs in the overall context of the struggle in France and Belgium. One of the most significant results of the French mutinies was that, from the summer of 1917, the British and Dominion forces under Haig had to shoulder the main burden of responsibility for Allied offensive operations on the Western Front.

Mines and method at Messines

Haig's plan for the BEF's Flanders offensive, as presented to a conference of his Army commanders on 7 May, split the projected operations into two stages. The first would consist of an attack on the Wytschaete-Messines Ridge, south of Ypres, around 7 June. The second, taking place some weeks later, would be a 'Northern Operation' designed to capture the Passchendaele-Staden Ridge and Gheluvelt plateau to the east of Ypres before seizing the Thourout-Roulers railway link and then clearing the Belgian coast, aided by an amphibious landing. It was regarded as essential to take Messines Ridge first in order to guarantee a secure defensive flank for the subsequent advance east of Ypres and also to provide elbow-room south and south-west of Ypres for the assembly of the guns and troops needed for the attack in the centre and on the left of the Salient. Although General Sir Herbert Plumer knew the Salient better than any of his other Army commanders, Haig believed that he was too careful and deliberate to lead the main operation, which was handed to the more thrustful Gough. Plumer's Second Army

ABOVE General Sir Herbert Plumer (left) with Field
-Marshal Sir Douglas Haig (right). (IWM)

BELOW Australian troops studying a contour model of
Messines Ridge, 6 June 1917. (IWM)

would instead carry out the preliminary
assault against Messines Ridge.

With his ruddy face, white moustache and
corpulent figure, Plumer had the appearance
of an elderly country squire rather than a
successful general, but few could match his
profound understanding of the principles
of modern trench warfare or his concern
to minimise casualties. Plumer and
Major-General Charles Harington, his Chief
of Staff, were a formidable team, whose
watchwords were 'Trust, Training and
Thoroughness'. Typically, their meticulous
preparations for the Messines operation
included the construction of an enormous
contour model of the Ridge. Seventy-two new
Mark IV tanks were made available to Second
Army, which could also call upon 2,266 guns.
For the latter, a methodical barrage and
counter-battery programme was planned,
special attention being paid to the problems
arising from the current German tactics of
deep defence and counter-attack. The
bombardment would commence on 21 May.
The feature which made the Messines attack
particularly memorable, however, was the
digging of 24 huge mines under the German
front defences. Some of the mines had been
initiated more than 12 months earlier. On
the day of the attack the mines would be

A German pillbox which has been overturned by one of the mines at Factory Farm, Messines Ridge, 1917. (IWM)

blown immediately before the infantry assault. The task of taking the northern sector of the Ridge was assigned to X Corps; the central sector, including Wytschaete village, would be secured by IX Corps; and II Anzac Corps was ordered to seize the southern shoulder of the Ridge and Messines itself.

Nineteen of the mines, containing nearly 1,000,000 lbs of high explosive in all, were detonated at 3.10 am on 7 June 1917. The nine assaulting divisions, advancing behind a creeping barrage, rapidly overcame those bewildered German defenders who had survived in the outpost and forward zones. Demonstrating that they had profited from painstaking battle rehearsals, from the lessons of the Somme and from the recent success at Vimy Ridge, the British and Dominion assault troops contrived to outflank or surround many German pillboxes, machine-gun posts and other strongpoints, which were subsequently cleared by trained mopping-up parties. By mid-morning, having suffered comparatively

light losses, Plumer's Second Army held the crest of the Ridge. During the afternoon the advance continued against the Oosttaverne Line, which ran across the eastern, or reverse, slope of the Ridge. At this stage casualties began to increase as the Ridge became overcrowded and, in the II Anzac Corps sector on the right, some units were even fired upon by their own artillery. However, the Oosttaverne Line was totally in Second Army's grasp after four days and all gains were consolidated within a week. The storming of Messines Ridge cost the BEF some 25,000 officers and men while German casualties were approximately 23,000, of whom 10,000 were missing.

The Messines attack, like that at Vimy Ridge, was, in most respects, a model set-piece assault, yet it also resembled the April success in the BEF's failure to follow up a brilliant initial victory. Haig and Plumer were both aware of the chance to gain ground on the western end of the Gheluvelt plateau – a possibility which the Germans themselves recognised and feared – but Plumer informed Haig on 8 June that he would require three days to bring his artillery forward. An impatient Haig thereupon transferred two of Plumer's corps to the Fifth Army and instructed Gough to prepare the operation. Ironically, Gough – possibly recalling the unfortunate outcome of his own impetuosity at Bullecourt – feared that a preliminary attack towards Gheluvelt might produce nothing more than a vulnerable minor salient on his right flank. After taking longer to study the problem than the three-day delay requested by Plumer, Gough, on 14 June, counselled against such an operation and advocated a simultaneous attack along his *entire* front, six weeks later, on the opening day of the main offensive. Since the German defences on the plateau had already been strengthened during the pause, Haig weakly agreed to the further postponement of the Gheluvelt attack – a decision that he and the BEF would shortly come to regret.

Drowned hopes: The third battle of Ypres

Haig's Flanders plan had received the War Cabinet's *general* approval in mid-May on the understanding that the French would similarly be taking offensive action. Now that the latter could no longer be counted upon, Lloyd George believed that it would be folly for the BEF to attack virtually on its own. Haig, however, still confidently anticipated decisive results in 1917 and there were sound strategic reasons for sticking with his scheme. The Americans were far from ready and Russian military power was nearing collapse, so there was a distinct possibility that the Germans would regain the strategic initiative and administer a fatal blow to the French Army if the BEF failed to maintain the pressure. At the very least, Haig asserted, the German Army would suffer further attrition and become easier to defeat in 1918. Haig and Robertson therefore saw considerable risks in the projected transfer of divisions to Italy, a policy which could only weaken Allied strength on the Western Front. As shipping losses to U-boats

remained perilously high, Haig's scheme to clear the Flanders coast was given powerful support by the First Sea Lord, Admiral Jellicoe. These arguments notwithstanding, Lloyd George's War Cabinet did not finally authorise Haig's 'Northern Operation' until 21 July, by which time the preliminary bombardment had already been in progress five days. Haig was informed, moreover, that the offensive might well be terminated should casualties be judged to outweigh tangible achievements.

Not all the problems Haig experienced during the Third Battle of Ypres were of his own making. Since the digging of deep trenches was ruled out by the boggy Ypres terrain, General von Arnim's German Fourth Army based its defence upon concrete pillboxes and fortified farms behind a thinly-occupied forward zone. The pillboxes were built above ground, were sited to support each other with interlocking fire and were thick enough to withstand anything less weighty than 8-inch howitzer shells. The expert defensive tactician von Lossberg was made von Arnim's Chief of Staff on 13 June. Then, on 10 July, the Germans carried out a pre-emptive bombardment and attack in the Nieuport sector which badly disrupted preparations for a planned coastal advance by the British Fourth Army. The projected British amphibious landing was subsequently postponed and later dropped. Two serious mistakes can, however, be attributed to Haig. His first major error was to hand the leading role in the main offensive to Gough, thus delaying the 'Northern Operation' while the Fifth Army got into position; the second was his failure to insist on the capture of the western part of the Gheluvelt plateau before the principal attack.

Unhappily for the BEF, Haig compounded these mistakes by allowing Gough to prepare a battle plan that was far too ambitious. At the end of June Haig was envisaging a swift breakthrough but, as the opening of the offensive drew closer, he began to favour a step-by-step offensive consisting of a succession of limited advances. Because Haig tended to avoid discussing operational plans

British stretcher-bearers carrying a wounded man through knee-deep mud, near Boesinghe, 1 August 1917. (IWM)

fully with his Army commanders, Gough was left with the unfortunate impression that a rapid breakthrough was still the priority. Consequently he proposed that, on the first day, his Fifth Army should attempt a deep advance of 6,000 yards, penetrating beyond the main concentration of German field batteries to the German third line. If resistance proved light, the attacking troops should push on to a fourth objective. At this point there would be a pause of two to three days while artillery was moved up to support an assault against the Passchendaele Ridge, scheduled for the fourth day of the offensive. As was his custom, Haig deferred to the commander on the spot, permitting Gough's unrealistic plan to stand. Haig *did* remind Gough of the vital importance of securing the Gheluvelt plateau but failed to hammer home the point when it emerged that Gough's scheme laid insufficient emphasis on its capture. In these respects, the preparations for the Ypres offensive were reminiscent of those for the Somme in 1916, for the BEF was again about to begin a major attack with ambiguous objectives and a faulty plan. The ground selected by Haig for the offensive was unsuitable and, because it was largely under German observation, necessitated a lengthy British artillery bombardment if the German batteries were to be suppressed. The preparations for the Third Battle of Ypres thus involved a reversion to artillery tactics that were now nearly obsolete and, to make an unpromising situation worse, the protracted bombardment ruined the already fragile drainage of the area, helping to create a swampy landscape that made rapid movement extremely unlikely, if not impossible.

Supported by 2,936 guns, including some artillery from the British Second and French First Armies, nine divisions from Gough's Fifth Army began their assault at 3.50 am on 31 July. On their left two divisions of the French First Army struck between Steenstraat and Boesinghe. Units of the Second Army also attacked on their right. The initial results were heartening as much of Pilckem Ridge fell and the seizure of key observation points there and at the western extremity of the Gheluvelt plateau robbed the Germans of advantages they had enjoyed since May 1915. Plumer's troops took Hollebeke and the German

outpost line west of the Lys while the French captured Steenstraat and reached the outskirts of Bixschoote. However, in the crucial Gheluvelt plateau sector the British II Corps struggled to progress beyond the German first line. Of the 48 fighting tanks allotted to II Corps only 19 went into action and a gun firing from inside a massive pillbox which commanded the Menin Road east of Hooge accounted for most of these. The setback in this sector effectively halved the Fifth Army's attack frontage. The rain which appeared during the afternoon changed from a drizzle to a persistent downpour soon after 4pm, greatly reducing visibility. In several places German counter-attacks drove the British back and, by 2 August, the continuing bad weather had forced the British to suspend operations. The initial assault had carried the Fifth Army forward about 3,000 yards but, disappointingly, Gough's divisions were still a long way short of their first-day objectives.

The persistent rain largely precluded any more major advances that month. The

'Hell Fire Corner' on the Menin Road, one of the most dangerous spots in the Ypres Salient. (IWM)

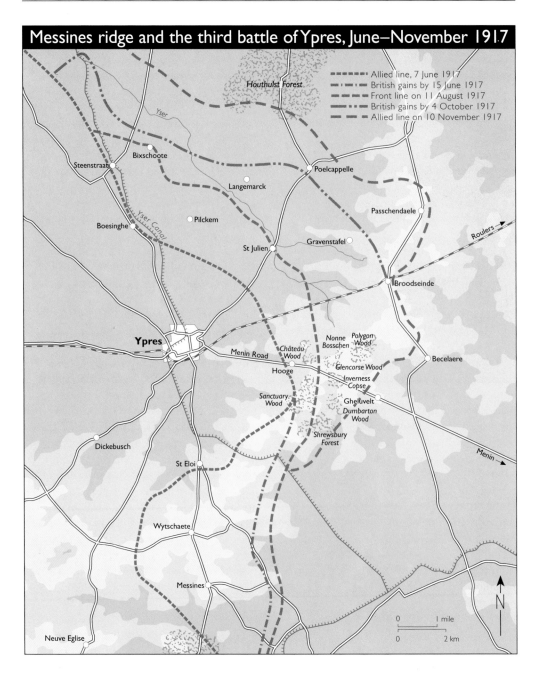

Messines ridge and the third battle of Ypres, June–November 1917

Houthulst Forest

- ▬ ▬ ▬ Allied line, 7 June 1917
- ▬ · ▬ · ▬ British gains by 15 June 1917
- ▬ ▬ ▬ Front line on 11 August 1917
- ▬ · · ▬ British gains by 4 October 1917
- ▬ ▬ ▬ Allied line on 10 November 1917

Yser

Bixschoote

Steenstraat

Poelcappelle

Langemarck

Passchendaele

Yser Canal

Pilckem

Boesinghe

Roulers

Gravenstafel

St Julien

Broodseinde

Ypres

Nonne   Polygon
Bosschen   Wood

Menin Road   Château
Wood

Glencorse Wood

Becelaere

Hooge

Inverness
Copse

Sanctuary
Wood

Gheluvelt
Dumbarton
Wood

Shrewsbury
Forest

Dickebusch

Menin

St Eloi

Wytschaete

Messines

N

0   1 mile

0   2 km

Neuve Eglise

Ypres Salient was transformed into a gloomy
expanse of mud and water-filled craters. All
troops moving up to the front line had to
negotiate treacherous duckboard tracks or
plank roads that were targeted by enemy
gunners. The Fifth Army took Langemarck
on 16 August but two more attempts to seize
the Gheluvelt plateau proved abortive,
despite heavy fighting at Inverness Copse

and Glencorse Wood close to the Menin
Road. On 25 August Haig belatedly rectified
his earlier mistake by transferring the leading
role in the battle, as well as the frontage of
II Corps, to Plumer and the Second Army.

While Haig resisted pressure from Lloyd
George to halt the bogged-down offensive,
Plumer was given three weeks to prepare the
next step and used the opportunity to

Wounded being treated at an advanced dressing station near Ypres, 20 September 1917. (IWM)

introduce more flexible assault tactics. Attacks would be led by lines of skirmishers, followed by small teams of infantry deployed loosely to outflank strongpoints and pillboxes. Each such group, with its own Mills bombers, Lewis gunners and rifle grenadiers, would fight as a self-contained unit. Other small groups, acting as mopping-up parties, would bring up the rear. Fresh reserves of infantry would be kept ready to deal with the expected German counter-attacks, which would also be subjected to intense, well-planned artillery fire and machine-gun barrages.

Plumer's methodical, step-by-step attacks with limited objectives – helped by a period of dry weather – immediately made some headway in the sub-battles of the Menin Road Ridge (20–25 September) and Polygon Wood (26 September–3 October). A distinguished contribution to these operations was made by I Anzac Corps, the Australians clearly being far happier under

Plumer's command than they had been under Gough. The impact of these attacks was shown by the fact that, in the Salient, the Germans were now obliged to modify their elastic defence system and again hold forward positions in greater strength, thereby making themselves more vulnerable to Plumer's artillery. On 4 October, II Anzac Corps joined in Plumer's *third* attack, which aimed to capture Broodseinde Ridge and the eastern end of the Gheluvelt plateau. The British X Corps drove the last German defenders from Polygon Wood and the New Zealand Division took Gravenstafel but, although the main objectives were gained, rain yet again turned the battlefield into a morass, making exploitation impossible.

Some sources maintain that Plumer and Gough advocated stopping the offensive at this point, though documentary evidence to support this claim is difficult to find. Haig certainly wanted to reach the Passchendaele Ridge to provide a firm line for the approaching winter and decided to continue operations for another month. Conditions in the Salient were now so appalling that men

ABOVE Men of the Lancashire Fusiliers carrying
duckboards forward over muddy ground near Pilckem,
10 October 1917. (IWM)

BELOW View of the Passchendale battlefield in
November 1917. (IWM)

were drowning in liquid mud. On
6 November the Canadian Corps took the
mound of pulverised rubble that had once
been Passchendaele, the village that has
since lent its name to the whole Third Battle

of Ypres – which itself has come to symbolise all the worst horrors of the Great War. When the Flanders offensive finally ended on 10 November, both sides had suffered losses of approximately 250,000, though, for the British, these casualties were less than those incurred on the Somme and represented a lower daily average than at Arras in the spring of 1917. Despite an advance of some five miles and Plumer's impressive September operations, none of Haig's distant objectives had been attained and even the northernmost tip of Passchendaele Ridge remained in German hands.

Massed tanks at Cambrai

Although its morale and manpower were stretched almost to breaking point by the fighting at Ypres, the BEF nevertheless made one more offensive effort in 1917. On 20 November, at Cambrai, the British concentrated their tanks so that, for the first time, they were deployed for a mass attack rather than scattered in small groups along the front for local infantry support.

The assault at Cambrai evolved from a Tank Corps plan for a large-scale raid, the chief object of which was *not* to seize ground but to deal the Germans a bruising blow on terrain which, unlike the Ypres Salient, actually suited tanks. Byng and the Third Army staff expanded the scheme between August and November, transforming it into a major operation against the Hindenburg Line. Both Haig and Byng perceived advantages in a plan which might not only rebuild the BEF's reputation and revive morale but also simultaneously draw the enemy's gaze from the Italian Front, where the Italians had suffered a near-catastrophic defeat at Caporetto on 24 October. Third Army hoped to pierce the Hindenburg system between the Canal du Nord and the Canal de l'Escaut before sending cavalry through the breach to secure crossings over the Sensée and isolate Cambrai. Infantry and tanks, after taking Bourlon Wood, were then to clear the Germans from Cambrai and the area between the principal waterways. It would be up to GHQ to decide the next step, possibly a drive towards Douai and Valenciennes. The main drawback was that the attrition at Ypres and the demands of the Italian Front left the BEF with scanty reserves for any exploitation at Cambrai. In short, the plan had outgrown the resources which the

BEF possessed in late 1917. Nor was it helped by Byng's desire to employ all the available tanks and infantry divisions in the breakthrough phase.

On the positive side, the plan combined some promising tactical elements. These included the decision to abandon the customary long artillery preparation and to permit the 1,003 supporting guns to deliver a surprise hurricane bombardment, capitalising on the new technique of 'predicted' shooting without prior registration of targets. Another novel aspect was the drill for tank-infantry co-operation developed by the Tank Corps and endorsed by Byng. Three hundred and seventy-eight fighting tanks, all carrying large brushwood bundles or 'fascines' to assist them in crossing trenches, would operate in groups of three. In each group, an 'advanced guard' tank would move 100 yards ahead of the two main body tanks, its task being to subdue German fire and protect the two following tanks. The latter would lead infantry sections through the German wire

British tanks moving forward at Graincourt for the attack on Bourlon Wood, near Cambrai, 23 November 1917. (IWM)

and over the opposing trenches. Ninety-eight supporting tanks carried supplies, bridging material, telephone cables, wireless or grapnels for hauling aside barbed wire. Moreover, the British – profiting from the lessons of Third Ypres – made greater use of low-flying aircraft to strike German artillery and troops.

The opening assault, by six of Byng's 19 infantry divisions, was made along a six-mile sector at 6.20 am on 20 November 1917. The surprise achieved by the sudden bombardment and the employment of massed tanks enabled Byng's formations, in most places, to break through the Hindenburg front and support systems to a depth of three to four miles. However, in the left centre, the 51st (Highland) Division failed to take the key village of Flesquières on the first day. Many of its accompanying tanks either broke down short of the objective or were disabled by German gunners who had been specially trained in anti-tank defence. By 23 November only 92 tanks remained operational and, because the British cavalry were disappointingly unable to exploit the initial breach, the old problem of maintaining the impetus of an advance beyond the assault phase again appeared to defy solution.

Over the next few days the Third Army was involved in what was essentially a fierce infantry battle for Bourlon Ridge, west of Cambrai. For all their efforts, the British divisions never completely secured Bourlon village or the neighbouring Bourlon Wood and, after a week, were left holding a salient nine miles wide and four to five miles deep. On 30 November, the German Second Army, commanded by General von der Marwitz, launched a savage counter-stroke against this salient. The Germans similarly opted for a short bombardment, using smoke, gas and high-explosive shells, and also employed large numbers of aircraft for ground-attack duties. The German counter-blow was perhaps most notable for the vital part played by storm troops, employing assault and infiltration tactics developed during the past two years. The timely arrival of some British reinforcements slowed German

progress but, at Haig's insistence, Byng fell back to a shorter, and more defensible, line in front of Flesquières by 5–6 December, thereby abandoning much of the ground originally gained. Casualties at Cambrai totalled more than 40,000 on each side but the most significant feature of the battle was the fact that both the British and Germans achieved a measure of success with tactical methods which at last seemed to offer a way out of the long-standing deadlock.

Taking stock

Victory had proved as elusive as ever for the Allies in 1917. Nivelle's failure, the French Army mutinies, the misery of the Passchendaele mud and the late setback after the brilliant initial success at Cambrai all combined to cast a dark cloud over Allied hopes for the immediate future. The war correspondent Philip Gibbs observed that, for the first time in the war, 'the British Army lost its spirit of optimism, and there was a sense of deadly depression among the many officers and men with whom I came in

Young British conscripts photographed at the infantry base deport at Etaples in 1918. (IWM)

touch'. However, a brief mutiny at the infantry base depot at Etaples in September was caused by poor accommodation and a brutal training régime at that particular camp and did *not* signal a major collapse in morale throughout the BEF. The losses in the attrition battles at Arras and Ypres provided Lloyd George with yet more ammunition to use against Haig. Indeed, the news, in December 1917, that Allenby had captured Jerusalem from the Turks appeared to buttress the position of those who argued against the primacy of the Western Front. While still unwilling to provoke a political crisis by removing Robertson and Haig, Lloyd George continued to seek ways of limiting their authority and influence.

Pétain's judicious blend of discipline and reform had brought the French Army back from the edge of the abyss into which it had stared during the spring and early summer but, in spite of its praiseworthy performance in limited operations at Verdun in August and the Chemin des Dames in October, nobody

was sure how it would fare if called upon to mount large-scale attacks. Pétain himself remained reluctant to risk such offensives until the Americans arrived in force.

So far, the assembly of United States troops had proceeded at a frustratingly slow pace. By 1 December 1917 barely four American divisions had reached France. Furthermore, General John Joseph 'Black Jack' Pershing, who commanded the American Expeditionary Force (AEF), had been strictly enjoined to keep his formations together as a distinct national army and to resist any attempt to use them merely as reinforcements for weakened French and British units. On a more constructive note, the establishment of a Supreme War Council at Versailles in November 1917 promised improved co-ordination of Allied strategy in the coming year.

The German Army had some reasons for optimism, at least in the short term, at the

American soldiers about to disembark at Liverpool. (IWM)

end of 1917. The new artillery and storm-troop assault tactics tested in operations at Riga, Caporetto and Cambrai had proved highly effective. The German formations on the Western Front were therefore retrained during the winter and were simultaneously augmented by divisions released from the Eastern Front following the Bolshevik Revolution in Russia in November. A sobering factor, however, was the knowledge that the Allied blockade was causing serious shortages of oil, petrol, rubber, horses and fodder, all of which would reduce the German Army's own ability to sustain mobile operations over long periods in 1918. Ominously, troops of a previously dependable division had stopped to loot a British supply depot during the German counter-stroke at Cambrai on 30 November.

1917 had certainly not been a year of total gloom for Haig and the BEF. The technical and tactical strides made by the BEF during the past 12 months were evident in the advance of XVII Corps and the success of the Canadian Corps at Arras and Vimy Ridge on 9 April; in the storming of Messines Ridge on 7 June; in Plumer's powerful blows at Ypres in late September; and in the breaking of the Hindenburg Line near Cambrai in November. Even the clinging mud of Passchendaele could not wholly obscure the achievements resulting from the BEF's collective improvement and learning process since the Somme.

Germany plans to attack

As 1917 ended, the Allies knew that they must expect a major German offensive in the west early the following year. In December 1917 both Russia and Romania suspended hostilities with the Central Powers, enabling Germany to speed up the transfer of units from the Eastern Front. Thirty-three divisions were moved to France and Belgium before 1918 dawned. The Allies, in contrast, faced severe manpower problems. Six French divisions were sent to Italy and another three were disbanded, reducing the total of French divisions on the

Western Front to 100, each with an infantry strength of no more than 6,000.

The BEF was in similar difficulties. Haig requested 334,000 reinforcements but had only acquired just over 174,000 by 21 March 1918. Lloyd George, who bore the responsibility for ensuring that Britain's *industrial* manpower resources remained equal to the demands of the war, undoubtedly believed that the holding back of men in Britain might make it easier for him to limit wasteful offensives. Haig, in turn, could argue that too many men had been diverted to what *he* saw as peripheral campaigns or 'sideshows'. However, recent scholarship indicates that the general reserve was kept in Britain by Robertson and the War Office rather than by the Prime Minister and that Haig himself may have inadvertently encouraged this policy by asserting that he could withstand a German offensive for at least 18 days with his existing forces. The manpower shortage *did* mean that, in February and March 1918, most BEF divisions were reduced from 12 battalions to nine, although the New Zealand Division, the four Canadian divisions and the five Australian divisions all retained the 12-battalion organisation. Of the British formations on the Western Front, 115 battalions were broken up, seven were converted into Pioneer battalions and 38 were amalgamated to form 19 battalions.

Little immediate assistance would be forthcoming from the Americans. Pershing had only 130,000 troops in France by 1 December 1917 and all AEF divisions would require three months' additional training on arrival. For a short period early in 1918, therefore, the Germans would enjoy the rare luxury of outnumbering the Franco-British forces, deploying 192 divisions against 156.

Acknowledging that the convoy system and air cover were now helping Britain to counter the U-boat threat, Germany's military leaders decided to seize their last real opportunity for a decisive victory on the Western Front before American strength became overwhelming. Ludendorff consequently planned to unleash a

Kaiserschlacht ('Imperial Battle') of successive, inter-related attacks that would together hasten the collapse of 'the whole structure' of the Allied armies. He judged that, if the British and Dominion forces were defeated, the others would inevitably capitulate in their wake. The initial German blow would therefore be delivered mainly against the BEF. After all the possibilities had been discussed during the winter, three, in particular, appeared to meet Ludendorff's criteria. One such attack, code-named *George*, would aim to break through the front near Armentières, in Flanders, and advance against Hazebrouck, taking the British forces to the north from the flank and rear. A subsidiary operation, *George II*, would isolate and overcome the BEF's units in the Ypres Salient. The second possible attack, *Mars*, would be directed against Arras. The third, *Michael*, would involve a powerful blow against the British Third and Fifth Armies on either side of St Quentin, between Arras and La Fère. As soon as the British defences in this sector were breached, German forces could wheel north and push the BEF back towards the sea. It was obviously advisable to launch the Flanders assault in dry conditions, which might not occur until April or May, and the BEF's positions at Arras were considered too tough an obstacle for the opening attack, so, on 21 January, Ludendorff settled upon *Michael* as his first choice for the principal offensive in the spring. After another seven weeks of detailed planning, 21 March was selected as the start date.

In the final plan, Crown Prince Rupprecht's Army Group would provide the right-wing forces, namely General Otto von Below's Seventeenth Army and General von der Marwitz's Second Army. These were to attack south of Arras and pinch out the British-held Flesquières salient, near Cambrai. They would next push on towards Péronne and Bapaume, across the 1916 Somme battlefield, to a line between Arras and Albert before swinging north-west, enveloping Arras as they advanced. On their left, General von Hutier's Eighteenth Army, from the Army Group of Crown Prince Wilhelm, would attack across the River Somme and the Crozat Canal to protect the flank of the right-wing armies, deal with any French reserves moving up from the south and drive a wedge between the French and British forces. The Eighteenth Army might also help von der Marwitz around Péronne if required. *Mars* could proceed once the necessary tactical success *south* of Arras had been attained. Ludendorff meanwhile permitted planning for *George* to continue, just in case *Michael* failed to live up to hopes and expectations.

A major retraining programme was instituted during the winter in an attempt to acquaint more units with the tactics developed by the élite assault units, or storm troops, over the previous two years. Approximately one-quarter of German infantry divisions were designated 'attack divisions' (*angriffsdivisionen*) and received the best new equipment and weapons, including light machine-guns. The remainder, primarily responsible for holding the line, were classified as 'trench divisions'

Crown Prince Rupprecht of Bavaria. (IWM)

Operation *Michael*: The plan

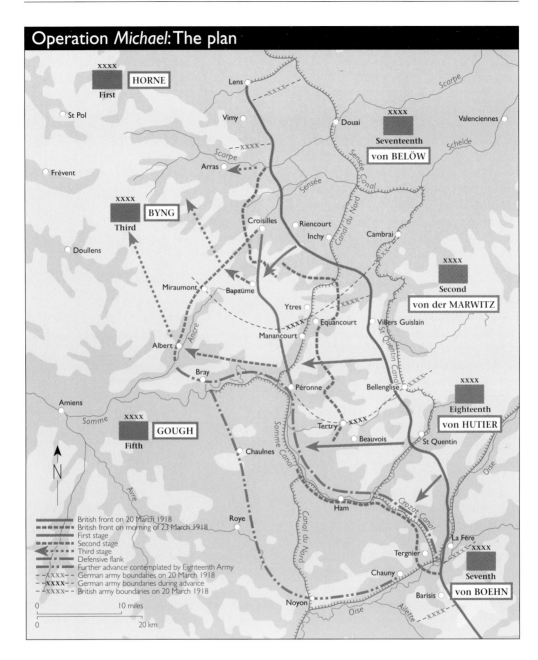

Legend:
- British front on 20 March 1918
- British front on morning of 23 March 1918
- First stage
- Second stage
- Third stage
- Defensive flank
- Further advance contemplated by Eighteenth Army
- German army boundaries on 20 March 1918
- German army boundaries during advance
- British army boundaries on 20 March 1918

0   10 miles
0   20 km

(stellungsdivisionen). Storm troops were assigned a key role in *Michael*, their task being to probe for weak spots in the opposing defences and to cause as much confusion as possible in rear areas through infiltration and envelopment. However, the artillery was arguably the most important element in the initial assault phase. The Germans would employ the gunnery methods tested and refined at Riga,

Caporetto and Cambrai by such experts as Colonel Georg Bruchmüller, who was himself now attached to the Eighteenth Army and shaped the whole artillery plan for *Michael*. His scrupulously-orchestrated fire plans were founded upon brief hurricane bombardments of prodigious intensity and weight, employing 'predicted' shooting techniques. Great care was taken to disrupt communications and concentration areas

German storm troops cross a wire entanglement during training at Sedan, 1917. (IWM)

deep behind Allied lines, while a high proportion of gas shells was incorporated to neutralise and suppress enemy gunners.

With its formations not only weakened by recent battles and reorganisation but also containing large numbers of raw conscripts, the BEF was hardly in the ideal condition to resist the approaching German onslaught. Although Haig remained in command, several of his senior staff officers – including Kiggell, his Chief of Staff, and Charteris, his Chief of Intelligence – had been replaced. At home, Robertson resigned as CIGS when Lloyd George tried to restrict his authority by nominating General Sir Henry Wilson as British representative on the 'Executive War Board' of the Supreme War Council. To rub salt into the wound, it was Wilson who succeeded Robertson as Chief of the Imperial General Staff on 18 February.

Both Haig and Pétain, in December, had ordered the construction of systems which would allow their armies to adopt flexible defence in depth similar to that introduced by the Germans in 1916–1917. In the BEF's area it was intended that the system would embody Forward, Battle and Rear Zones, each comprising several successive lines of continuous trenches or groups of trenches besides mutually-supporting strongpoints and machine-gun posts sited for all-round defence. However, lack of time and labour shortages prevented the completion of the new positions. Not having fought a big defensive battle for well over two years, the BEF also required many more weeks than it was actually granted in order to absorb these alternative tactical ideas. The outlook was not improved by the fact that, since November, five divisions had been transferred to Italy under Plumer's command. Furthermore, in January 1918, the BEF had been called upon to take over an extra stretch of the Allied line. Its right flank now extended to Barisis, over 20 miles south of St Quentin.

Gough's Fifth Army, which held the BEF's southernmost sector, possessed only three cavalry and 12 infantry divisions to defend 42 miles, in contrast to the Third Army, on its left, which could deploy 14 divisions to defend 28 miles. The positions which Gough's troops took over from the French were rudimentary and, in any event, not all of Gough's subordinates had entirely grasped the principles of elastic defence in depth. In consequence, the Fifth Army's Forward Zone was too densely occupied when the attack came.

Albeit with the advantages of hindsight, one can fairly accuse Haig of having miscalculated the possible direction and

weight of the German offensive, of being over-optimistic about the BEF's current defensive capabilities and of having underestimated the potential threat to the Fifth Army. There were admittedly few vital strategic objectives immediately behind Gough's front and east of Amiens, giving the Fifth Army more room to fall back and manoeuvre but it remains a matter of debate whether Haig was right to leave the Fifth Army quite so weak. All things considered, however, Haig was undoubtedly wise to keep most of his troops in the north, ensuring the security of Flanders and the Channel ports.

Michael

Bruchmüller's devastating prelude to Operation *Michael* began at 4.40 am on 21 March 1918, when 6,473 guns and 3,532 trench mortars opened fire. The infantry assault commenced in thick fog five hours later. Ninetten divisions of the German Seventeenth Army struck the British Third Army and 43 divisions of the German Second and Eighteenth Armies attacked Gough's Fifth Army. German shelling of British rear areas severely hampered communications, while the extensive employment of gas

Troops of the German Eighteenth Army massing in St Quentin, March 1918. (IWM)

largely subdued British batteries. Most of the defenders in the British Forward Zone were swiftly overrun. The fog that morning provided excellent cover for the infiltration tactics of the storm troops and prevented the British from bringing the full weight of their own artillery and machine-gun fire to bear on them as they approached and penetrated the main Battle Zone. In such conditions, those manning the British redoubts and strongpoints were left isolated and incapable of supporting each other.

The British front rapidly crumbled in many places, particularly on the Fifth Army's right in the sector only recently taken over from the French. Here the Germans burst through the Battle Zone, prompting Gough to pull the threatened British III Corps back to the line of the Crozat Canal. However, the Germans were not equally successful in all sectors. On their right, von Below's Seventeenth Army – confronted by the more strongly-held and better-prepared positions

of Byng's Third Army – made less satisfactory progress. Having decided against attacking the Flesquières salient frontally, the Germans failed to pinch it out as quickly as they hoped. The Second Army, under von der Marwitz, was likewise unable to achieve the planned breakthrough along its whole assault front. Even so, Haig and his senior commanders could not escape the fact that the BEF was now experiencing its biggest defensive crisis since 1914. Although the Germans had suffered close to 40,000 casualties on the first day, the British too had lost over 38,000 men and around 500 guns. Worryingly, the British casualty total included 21,000 who had been taken prisoner, a sure sign that, for many weary units and individuals, the reservoir of courage and endurance had finally run dry.

On 22 March, the second day of the offensive, the British front continued to fall apart. The normally confident and resourceful General Maxse, misunderstanding Gough's intentions, was too hasty in ordering his own XVIII Corps to withdraw to the Somme, a move which compelled XIX Corps, on his left, to retire in conformity. In a similar fashion, the right of Byng's Third Army was increasingly exposed by the disintegration of the Fifth Army's front further south. Nevertheless, Byng can perhaps be faulted for delaying the evacuation of the Flesquières salient for the best part of three days, a decision which resulted in unnecessary losses in the 2nd and 63rd (Royal Naval) Divisions and also contributed to the opening of a yawning gap at the junction of the British Third and Fifth Armies.

By the third day, the Germans had pushed some elements of the Fifth Army back more than 12 miles and von Hutier's troops were thrusting westwards to secure crossings over the Crozat Canal and the Somme. As at other critical moments of the First World War, however, the Germans allowed unexpected but glittering tactical opportunities to deflect them from their original strategic aim. Thus, rather than reinforcing his stalled right wing to guarantee the success of the vital sweep to the north-west, Ludendorff strengthened the left. He also issued new orders which steered the Seventeenth Army towards Abbeville and St Pol and the Second Army westwards in the direction of Amiens. The Eighteenth Army – previously cast in the flank protection role – was to drive south-west towards Montdidier and Noyon in a much more deliberate effort to split the French and British armies. Instead of concentrating to administer a powerful left hook, the three German armies involved would, in essence, be moving in divergent directions.

Ludendorff's revised orders were based on the false assumption that the British Third and Fifth Armies would not recover. The BEF's immediate prospects were certainly bleak. Péronne was abandoned to the Germans on 23 March, and Bapaume was evacuated the following day. After the Fifth Army had retreated across the old Somme battlefield, Albert was lost on 26 March. The British Third Army, while largely maintaining a firm hold on its positions near Arras, was forced to draw back its right wing in order to stay in touch with the Fifth Army's left.

Whatever his intentions before 21 March, Haig was daily becoming ever more

Men of the 12th Battalion, The Rifle Brigade, with French troops in rifle pits near Nesle, 25 March 1918. (IWM)

German transport – mostly horse-drawn – on the Albert–Bapaume road, March 1918. (IWM)

conscious of the Fifth Army's predicament and of the growing threat to Amiens, a rail centre of paramount importance to the BEF. In this situation he was therefore doubly distressed to receive what he considered to be woefully insufficient support from the French. Always the pessimist, Pétain feared that the Germans might still launch a big offensive against the French in Champagne. Above all, he was concerned with the need to shield Paris and was consequently prepared, if circumstances demanded, to withdraw south-west to Beauvais, even though this would take the French forces further away from the BEF. To be fair to Pétain, there also appeared to be a strong

possibility that, if the situation deteriorated beyond repair, the BEF would retire to the north. On this occasion, however, Haig's desire for the French to cover Amiens, permitting him to retain enough reserves to protect the Channel ports, caused him to cast aside his normal objections to a unified command. Following appeals from Haig, an inter-Allied conference was hurriedly convened at Doullens on 26 March, when – again at Haig's insistence – Foch was given the necessary authority to co-ordinate the operations of the Allied armies on the Western Front. This was not an instant panacea, as the German Eighteenth Army's advance went on for a few more days, pushing the French out of Montdidier, yet Foch's appointment raised Allied morale and eased the pressure on Pétain and Haig. In addition, although French reserves did not arrive at once, there could no longer be any real doubt that the French would help to defend Amiens.

Ludendorff, whose handling of the offensive was increasingly erratic, had issued revised orders on 25 March, switching the main emphasis back to the right and centre. *Mars* – the attack against Arras – was launched on 28 April but was a costly failure. The awful truth for Ludendorff was that, when tested, the German Army was unable to sustain *prolonged* mobile operations in 1918. The German forces in France possessed a relatively small cavalry arm, no armoured cars and few tanks, while, after years of blockade, the horse-drawn and motorised transport they *did* have was not always up to the required standards. The heavy losses being suffered by the storm troops highlighted the widening gulf in quality between the élite assault formations and the 'trench divisions'. For all its skill, intellect

General (later Marshal) Ferdinand Foch at Sarcus, 17 May 1918. (IWM)

and professionalism, the German General Staff had too often become distracted by short-term organisational and operational matters and had ultimately created an unbalanced army that could not fulfil its principal strategic purpose. The pace of the advance was dictated by the capacity of its foot soldiers and, by the end of March 1918, the German infantryman was nearing exhaustion, though cases of drunkenness and looting were not confined to the German Army alone. In a vain attempt to inject new life into the offensive, Ludendorff tinkered with his plan for the third time in a week, reducing its scope to the comparatively limited objective of taking Amiens. The blow was parried at Villers Bretonneux, approximately 10 miles east of Amiens, on 4 and 5 April by the 9th Australian Brigade and units of the British 18th Division, 58th Division and 3rd Cavalry Division. This setback convinced Ludendorff that *Michael* would not repay further sacrifice and on 5 April, its 16th day, he terminated the offensive.

Since 21 March the Germans had advanced some 40 miles, regaining much of the territory they had occupied two years before but they had not achieved the decisive result they had sought. British casualties in this period totalled 178,000, including 70,000 prisoners, and the French had lost approximately 77,000. German casualties numbered approximately 250,000, the many lost storm troops proving particularly difficult to replace. In the BEF Gough was removed from command of the Fifth Army. Though the odds had been stacked against him, he had, in fact, conducted a deft fighting retreat during which the Fifth Army's line may have been badly bent but never fatally broken. Even so, he was singled out as the scapegoat for the Fifth Army's reverses and was succeeded on 28 March by General Sir Henry Rawlinson, who had spent the last month as British Military Representative at Versailles. In an apparent effort to wipe out the recent and unwarranted blot on its reputation, the Fifth Army was redesignated as the Fourth Army on 2 April.

Operation *Michael*: The end of the offensive

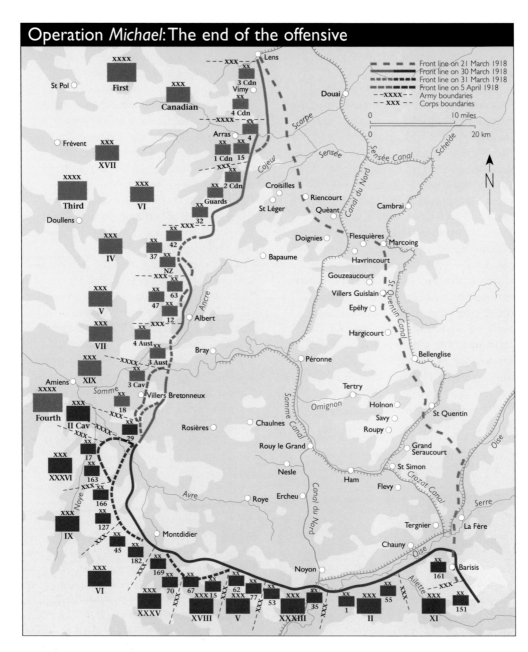

'With our backs to the wall'

Ludendorff's order for the Flanders offensive to go ahead was given even before *Michael* was terminated. This second offensive, however, was scaled down from the original plan, this being symbolised by the revision of its code-name to *Georgette*. The modified plan called for the Sixth Army, under General von Quast, to strike between

Givenchy and Armentières and drive north-west across the Lys valley in the direction of the important rail centre at Hazebrouck, which lay behind the junction of the British First and Second Armies. The following day, General Sixt von Arnim's Fouth Army was to attack further north towards Messines. While British defences on this front were better than those in Picardy on 21 March, the BEF's reserves were now dangerously thin. The Germans too were showing distinct signs of strain from the March fighting and the majority of their assault formations for *Georgette* were 'trench divisions' rather than 'attack divisions'.

After another classic Bruchmüller artillery bombardment, the Germans made early progress on 9 April, easily overcoming the feeble resistance of the dispirited 2nd Portuguese Division near Neuve Chapelle and advancing approximately three-and-a-half miles at relatively small cost. On 10 April, when von Arnim's Fourth Army added its weight to the offensive, Messines village fell and part of the Messines-Wytschaete Ridge was yielded to the Germans. The British also withdrew from Armentières, which was situated between the converging German thrusts. Despite the Doullens agreement, Haig's pleas to Foch for assistance seemed initially to go unheeded, though even Foch was finding it difficult to force a gloomy and grudging Pétain to release the necessary reserves. As the Germans

Portuguese troops holding breastworks near Laventie early in 1918. (IWM)

pushed on to within five miles of Hazebrouck, Haig knew that he again faced a crisis. On 11 April he issued a special Order of the Day, which stated:

There is no other course open to us but to fight it out. Every position must be held to the last man: there must be no retirement. With our backs to the wall and believing in the justice of our cause each one of us must fight on to the end.

In the course of the next few days, the arrival in Flanders of the British 5th and 33rd Divisions and the 1st Australian Division eased the crisis on the Lys, and on 14 April Foch was named General-in-Chief of the Allied Armies, an additional step towards genuine unity of command. Now that he had greater control over the handling of Allied reserves, Foch rapidly introduced a rotation system permitting British divisions to move to quiet French sectors and release French formations to buttress threatened parts of the Allied line. In the British Second Army's zone of operations, the French had relieved British units along nine miles of

A line of men, blinded by tear gas, at an advanced
dressing station near Béthune, 10 April 1918. (IWM)

front by 19 April. Unfortunately for Plumer,
who had returned from Italy to resume
command of the Second Army, this French
assistance came slightly too late. With the
Germans consolidating their hold on
Messines Ridge, Plumer was obliged to make
the agonising but tactically necessary
decision to abandon Passchendaele Ridge –
won at such high cost the previous autumn –
and, in an echo of May 1915, pulled his
forces back to a less vulnerable perimeter
closer to Ypres. The withdrawal was executed
with all the Second Army's usual efficiency
and thoroughness.

Ludendorff, meanwhile, was not only
becoming daily more desperate but was also
displaying increasing strategic inconsistency.
The next significant German blow was not
delivered in Flanders but took the form of a
second, and belated, strike towards Amiens.
This opened, on 24 April, with another
attack on Villers Bretonneux. The attack was
preceded by a brief artillery bombardment,

which included a mixture of mustard gas
and high-explosive shells, and was made in
dense fog. Supported by 13 A7V tanks, the
Germans quickly overwhelmed many of the
inexperienced young conscripts in the
British 8th Division, tore open a three-mile
gap in the defences and seized Villers
Bretonneux. In front of Cachy, three British
Mark IV tanks engaged three German A7Vs
in the first ever tank-versus-tank combat.
With negligible help from the French when
it was most needed, Rawlinson and his
subordinate commanders organised an
audacious counter-attack, which took place
that night. By dawn on 25 April – the third
anniversary of the Gallipoli landings – the
13th and 15th Australian Brigades, assisted
on the right by the British 18th and
58th Divisions, had driven the Germans back
eastwards and, in a brilliant enveloping
movement, had 'pinched out' Villers
Bretonneux, which was largely cleared of
the enemy by midday.

In Flanders the Allied defence had been
less resilient for the same day, 25 April, the
crack German Alpine Corps wrested

possession of Mount Kemmel from the French. It was to be the last meaningful German success in the *Georgette* operations. On 29 April, the Germans launched a final attack against British and French positions between Ypres and Bailleul but their gains were insignificant. Like *Michael* before it, *Georgette* had run out of steam and, late in the evening of 29 April, Ludendorff suspended the Flanders offensive. Yet again Ypres, Amiens and the Channel ports had been saved by the determined resistance of the Allies.

Blücher and *Gneisenau*

Both sides desperately needed a pause in operations after *Georgette*. For the three major armies, manpower was a critical problem. The Germans had suffered around 380,000 casualties since 21 March, while the British had lost almost 240,000 men and the French some 92,000. Nevertheless, the Germans, with 206 divisions against 160, retained the strategic initiative on the Western Front. Ten of the BEF's available divisions were deemed to be exhausted, eight of them being reduced, for a short period, to cadre strength with just 10 officers and 45 men per battalion. The American Expeditionary Force, of course, represented the long-term solution to the manpower difficulties currently being experienced by the Allies. By 1 May the AEF in France numbered 430,000 officers and men. Each American division, with 28,000 men, was two or three times the size of British or French divisions but, as yet, the US 1st Division alone had reached the front line.

The strength of the AEF increased spectacularly to more than 650,000 by the end of May. Although he relented a little during the successive crises of the spring and early summer, Pershing continued to rebuff attempts to incorporate American soldiers in British and French units and strove, as far as possible, to keep the AEF intact as a distinct component of the Allied forces, so that it could ultimately undertake offensive operations as a national army under its own commanders.

The British forces had unquestionably been badly hurt by the German March and April offensives but had survived these gigantic blows mostly without external assistance. As a result, the BEF's morale rapidly recovered from the trials of the past few months and its optimism correspondingly soared. In contrast, Ludendorff was disturbed by evidence of a sharp decline in the discipline and morale of German troops, many of whom now tended to loiter around captured Allied supply dumps. Indeed, certain divisions had shown a marked reluctance to attack during the recent operations on the Lys. Some influential figures in the German Army, including von Lossberg, expressed doubts concerning the wisdom of launching more offensives. Ludendorff conceded that the German Army could no longer sustain two simultaneous offensives and that delays between big attacks were inevitable while the great German artillery 'battering train' was redeployed. However, he also knew that Germany's numerical superiority would not last and he must therefore order further offensives to achieve the elusive victory before American manpower finally and irrevocably gave the Allies the strategic advantage. For Ludendorff, the main aim was still the defeat of the BEF in Flanders but, even during the closing stages of *Georgette*, he had already concluded that it was first necessary to draw French reserves away from that sector, in order to deprive Haig of their support at the decisive moment.

With this in mind, Ludendorff chose to unleash the next major offensive – code-named Operation *Blücher* – against the French along the Chemin des Dames on the Aisne. Prospects of a German success here were enhanced by the fact that General Duchêne, the commander of the French Sixth Army, had failed to apply Pétain's instructions regarding flexible defence in depth and had placed too many troops in forward positions. In a twist of fate, five battered British divisions had been moved to the Aisne to recuperate under Foch's rotation scheme and

The German offensives, March–July 1918

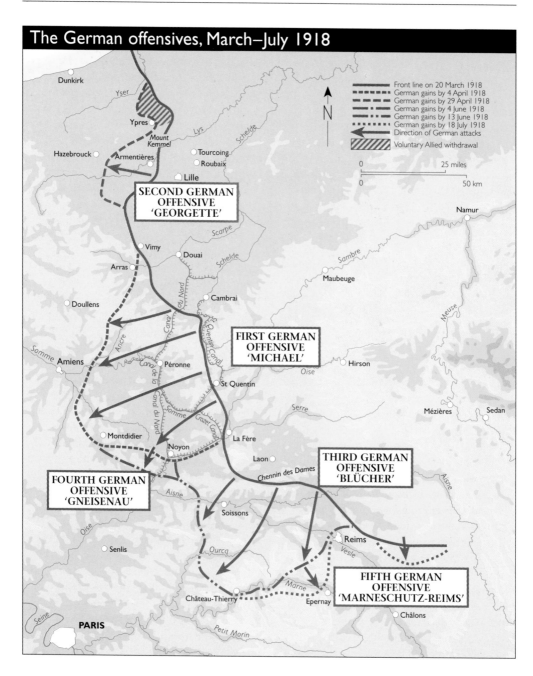

Front line on 20 March 1918
German gains by 4 April 1918
German gains by 29 April 1918
German gains by 4 June 1918
German gains by 13 June 1918
German gains by 18 July 1918
Direction of German attacks
Voluntary Allied withdrawal

SECOND GERMAN OFFENSIVE 'GEORGETTE'

FIRST GERMAN OFFENSIVE 'MICHAEL'

THIRD GERMAN OFFENSIVE 'BLÜCHER'

FOURTH GERMAN OFFENSIVE 'GNEISENAU'

FIFTH GERMAN OFFENSIVE 'MARNESCHUTZ-REIMS'

three of them – the 8th, 21st and 50th Divisions – were in the front line.

The German artillery plan for *Blücher* was once more prepared by the brilliant Bruchmüller, who had been nicknamed *Durchbruchmüller* ('Breakthrough Müller') by German soldiers. The 160-minute bombardment by nearly 4,000 guns which opened the Aisne offensive on 27 May was the densest yet in 1918 in terms of batteries per mile and has since been described as Bruchmüller's masterpiece. By the end of the first day eight French and British divisions had been virtually destroyed and the Germans had advanced some 12 miles – an amazing distance even in the changed conditions of 1918. On 28 May General von Boehn's Seventh Army seized Soissons and, by the evening of

German troops advancing through Pont Arcy, Aisne sector, 27 May 1918. (IWM)

30 May, had reached the Marne close to Château-Thierry, less than 60 miles from Paris.

Up to this point, *Blücher* had surpassed expectations, tempting the German High Command to forget that the offensive had been conceived primarily as a diversion. As Ludendorff pondered how best to capitalise upon von Boehn's dazzling progress, the Allies blocked the enemy advance. Ominously for the Germans, the United States 2nd and 3rd Divisions entered the line alongside the French in the battle for Château-Thierry. On 6 June, US Marines of the 2nd Division counter-attacked German forces at Belleau Wood. The Germans now occupied a deep salient which, because of its extended flanks, was tricky to defend. Damage to railways and roads also exacerbated German supply problems. Aiming to enlarge the salient, secure better defensive positions and suck in even more French reserves, Ludendorff launched a fourth offensive, code-named *Gneisenau*, towards the Matz between Noyon and

Montdidier. Here, like Duchêne on the Aisne, General Humbert, the commander of the French Third Army, had crowded too many troops into the forward zone. At the start of these operations on 9 June, the German Eighteenth Army, under von Hutier, once more achieved dramatic first-day gains, advancing around six miles. On 11 June, five divisions of General Mangin's French Tenth Army, with support from ground-attack aircraft and tanks, delivered a furious counter-stroke against von Hutier's left flank and brought *Gneisenau* to a shuddering halt. For Hindenburg and Ludendorff both time and strategic options were rapidly diminishing.

Hitting back

Despite halting the *Blücher* and *Gneisenau* offensives, the French had little cause for self-congratulation. The loss of the Chemin des Dames so soon after Foch's appointment as General-in-Chief had been a chastening experience while some members of Foch's own staff could scarcely conceal their mounting impatience with Pétain's pessimism and sluggish reactions. After coming near to collapse on the Aisne, the French were in no position to deride the BEF's recent performance in Picardy and Flanders. Haig's stock rose accordingly over the next few months, giving him greater influence in the shaping of Allied strategy and operations. At the same time, Ludendorff's problems worsened. In at least three of the four offensives to date he had permitted dazzling initial gains to distract him from his original strategic aim or to tempt him into continuing operations longer than was sensible. He was not the first to ignore the lesson that modern railway systems almost always enabled defenders to bring reserves to a crucial sector before the attackers could push sufficient men and equipment across the battlefield to exploit any breach. German combat troops remained capable of heroic endeavours but their morale had been progressively and irreparably damaged by the failure of four successive offensives. Their sufferings were magnified when, in June, the Spanish influenza pandemic of 1918–1919 started to exact its relentless and terrible toll on units already enfeebled by food shortages, further reducing the strength of German infantry formations.

The first American attack of the war had taken place as early as 28 May, when the US 1st Division seized Cantigny, near Montdidier. By 26 June American troops had also cleared Belleau Wood. In its operations at Cantigny, Belleau Wood and Château-Thierry, the AEF had incurred more than 11,000 casualties and fought with much the same mixture of patriotism, bravery and tactical inexperience that had characterised the BEF of July 1916. Symbolically, however, the Americans had faced hardened German units and had beaten them.

At Hamel, near Amiens, on 4 July, the Australian Corps carried out a model minor attack which offered the Allies equal, if not greater, encouragement for the future. Formed in November 1917 from the five Australian divisions on the Western Front, the Australian

Corps had been commanded since 31 May by Lieutenant-General Sir John Monash, who succeeded General Sir William Birdwood when the latter took over the reconstituted Fifth Army. A civil engineer before the war, Monash quickly demonstrated a capacity for painstaking and innovative operational planning that made him one of the BEF's most eminent corps commanders. Monash likened a modern battle plan to an orchestral score in which each 'instrument', or arm – artillery, tanks, aeroplanes and infantry – played a vital part in creating a harmonious whole. His insistence on teamwork and all-arms co-operation was keenly supported by the Fourth Army commander, Henry

Lieutenant-General Sir John Monash, who commanded the Australian Corps from May 1918. (IWM)

Rawlinson, who had himself learned from the brutal lessons of 1916 and was to handle his forces with distinction in the weeks and months to come.

In attacking at Hamel, Monash and Rawlinson hoped to remove a troublesome dent in the British line near Villers Bretonneux, thereby securing a straighter barrage line for future operations and depriving the Germans of a key vantage point on the spur above Hamel village. The battle plan embodied Monash's belief that infantry should no longer be expected to sacrifice themselves in bloody frontal assaults but should be given the maximum possible help by mechanised resources, including tanks, machine-guns, artillery, mortars and aircraft. Sixty new Mark V fighting tanks and 12 supply tanks were made available for the Hamel operation and special combined training gave the Australians a renewed trust in this weapon that had been absent since the bitter experience at Bullecourt in April 1917.

Monash was therefore able to economise on infantry, deploying only eight battalions – mainly from the 4th Australian Division – along a 6,000-yard front of attack. Any sound made by the tanks during their assembly would be deliberately drowned by the noise of artillery fire and aircraft and, in the assault, the tanks would advance level with the infantry under a creeping barrage.

With the attack scheduled for America's Independence Day, it was intended to use 10 companies of the US 33rd Division, then attached to the British Fourth Army for training. Almost at the last minute, Pershing refused to sanction their participation. The six rearmost companies were duly withdrawn but, to avoid further delays or disruption to the plan, Haig, Rawlinson and Monash stood firm with regard to the remaining four. In the event, the Australians and Americans captured all their objectives, together with

Men of the US 33rd Division resting near Corbie, 3 July 1918, before the attack at Hamel. (IWM)

1,472 prisoners and 171 machine-guns, in just over 90 minutes, at a cost of under 1,000 casualties. The supply of ammunition to forward troops by parachute was one of several elements of the Hamel plan which made it an invaluable blueprint for future set-piece assaults. Pershing, however, became more determined than ever to restrict or oppose French or British operational control of American formations.

Counter-stroke on the Marne

A strictly defensive strategy would have been the wisest course for Ludendorff to follow by early July. However, he still hoped to persuade the Allies to seek a peace settlement on terms favourable to Germany and, with this object in view, he decided to embark upon another offensive. The defeat of the BEF in Flanders remained his overriding objective but Ludendorff was aware of Allied strength there and chose instead to make a further attempt to lure Allied reserves to a different sector. To this end, on 15 July, the Germans struck either side of Reims. The German Seventh Army, commanded by von Boehn, encountered lively resistance from the US 3rd Division yet, by nightfall, had established a bridgehead four miles deep across the Marne. Von Mudra's First Army and von Einem's Third Army were far less successful east of Reims. On this front, General Gouraud's French Fourth Army had fully understood and applied Pétain's strictures about elastic defence and firmly checked German progress.

Three days later, on 18 July, the French and Americans delivered a major counter-stroke, which had been prepared by General Mangin, the aggressive commander of the French Tenth Army. With the French Sixth Army on their right, Mangin's units assailed the western face of the German salient between the Aisne and the Marne. The surprise counter-offensive was spearheaded by the US 1st and 2nd Divisions and supported by 225 tanks, a large proportion of which were new Renault light tanks. Within

48 hours the French Tenth Army pushed forward approximately six miles. By 6 August the Germans had suffered losses of 793 guns and 168,000 men, including 29,000 prisoners. Ludendorff's fifth and final gamble had ultimately proved as fruitless as its predecessors.

Like Moltke four years before, Ludendorff came close to nervous collapse in late July 1918. Increasingly erratic and uncertain, he was rapidly losing his grasp of strategic realities. Although the Germans no longer held the military initiative, Ludendorff refused to acknowledge that all hopes of offensive victories had vanished. He therefore spurned von Lossberg's shrewd advice that the German Army should withdraw to the relative security of the Hindenburg Line. Early in August he regained his composure to some degree, proposing a future policy whereby the German Army would return to its former defensive posture but would continue to sap Allied morale and manpower by making sudden small-scale attacks, in specially-selected sectors, from positions of considerable strength.

The black day of the German Army

The Germans were allowed no time to implement Ludendorff's revised strategy. The indefatigable Haig, whose single-mindedness contrasted sharply with Ludendorff's progressive instability, now sensed that Germany might, after all, be defeated in 1918. He had already obtained Foch's approval, in broad terms, of a plan submitted by Rawlinson for a larger-scale version of the Hamel attack, the chief aim this time being to eject the Germans from their positions between the Somme and the Avre and thus remove the lingering threat to Amiens. On 8 August, a few miles east of that city, Rawlinson's Fourth Army, with General Debeney's French First Army on its right, dealt the German Second and Eighteenth Armies a devastating blow. Ludendorff subsequently described 8 August 1918 as 'the black day of the German Army in the history of this war.'

Leading parts in the Allied attack were assigned to the Australian and Canadian Corps. Whereas British divisions were frequently switched from one corps or Army to another, the Australians and Canadians kept theirs together as distinct national bodies, making it easier for them to maintain high morale and to disseminate tactical

lessons learned on the battlefield. Had the movement of the Canadian Corps to the Amiens sector been detected, the Germans would have realised that an offensive was coming, and, to prevent this, two Canadian battalions remained in Flanders to generate false signals traffic. This measure – which would be echoed in the deception plans adopted before D-Day in 1944 – typified the secrecy which underpinned Rawlinson's

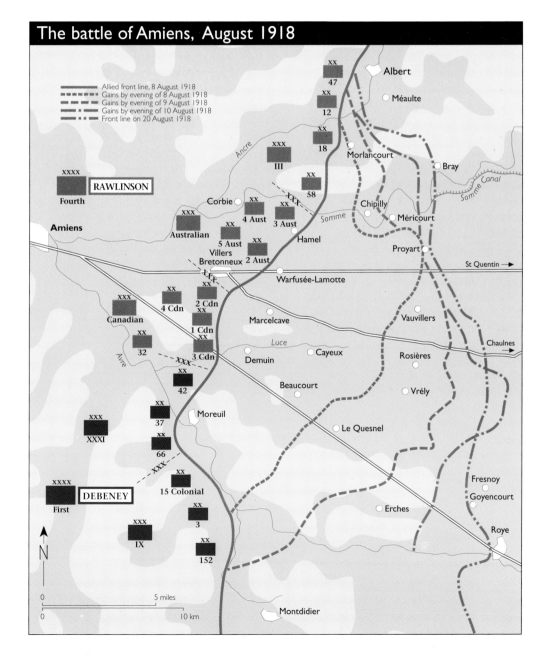

The battle of Amiens, August 1918

Allied front line, 8 August 1918
Gains by evening of 8 August 1918
Gains by evening of 9 August 1918
Gains by evening of 10 August 1918
Front line on 20 August 1918

assembly of the required men, weapons and equipment.

The Amiens attack also illustrated the progress wrought throughout the BEF in tactics and all-arms co-operation since the Somme offensive of 1916. The employment of aircraft in a ground-attack role, as well as on their normal artillery-spotting and reconnaissance duties, added extra bite to the offensive while more extensive use of wireless helped to improve battlefield communications. Three hundred and forty-two Mark V fighting tanks would lead the attack with the infantry, supported by 120 supply tanks, and, for the exploitation phase 72 of the lighter Medium Mark A 'Whippet' models were allotted to work with the cavalry. Infantry platoons – now generally comprising two half-platoons, each with Lewis gunners, riflemen and rifle grenadiers – were better able to adapt to the more fluid conditions of 1918 and, being more self-contained and possessing greater firepower than before, were capable of sustaining the momentum of the attack for longer periods. As at Hamel, however, the bedrock of Rawlinson's planning was the emphasis placed on teamwork.

A numbing surprise bombardment from 2,070 guns, arranged by the Fourth Army's chief gunner, Major-General C E D Budworth – Britain's answer to Bruchmüller –

announced the opening of the Amiens attack at 4.20 am on 8 August. This time the thick morning mist – so prevalent in Picardy – favoured the Allies. The preparations of the British III Corps, on the left, had been disrupted on 6 August, when the Germans reacted to an earlier Australian raid by counter-attacking near Morlancourt and were correspondingly more alert on this stretch of the front. Despite these unpropitious circumstances, III Corps managed to progress two miles, though its main thrust did not get beyond the first objective. The Australian Corps, in the centre, achieved a six-mile advance while the fresher Canadians – who had not been seriously engaged in the spring fighting – pushed forward up to eight miles. The progress of the French First Army, on the right of the Canadians, was less impressive. On 8 August the Germans lost 400 guns and 27,000 men, including 15,000 prisoners. The British Fourth Army's casualties were under 9,000.

By 12 August, as German resistance hardened in this sector, the Fourth Army's advance slowed. Only half a dozen British tanks were still in action. Nevertheless, the manner of the Allied victory at Amiens

A platoon of the 29th Battalion, Australian Imperial Force, in the morning mist at Warfusée-Lamotte, near Amiens, 8 August 1918. (IWM)

A Canadian 60-pounder battery in action,
10 August 1918. (IWM)

mattered more than its scale. The BEF's combat skills and confidence were growing daily at a time when the German Army as a whole was clearly in sharp decline. Their artillery and machine-gunners, and some individual German divisions, continued to fight with the old determination and professionalism but defences were no longer built or maintained with the same care and a morose and fatalistic mood had descended upon many units. As German reserves and reinforcements approached the line, they were now greeted with cries of 'You're prolonging the war!' or dubbed 'blacklegs' by troops being relieved.

Return to Albert and Bapaume

Bereft of confidence and long-term solutions following the Allied onslaught at Amiens, Ludendorff knew that the war must be ended. The Kaiser agreed and, at a conference at Spa on 14 August, instructed Admiral von Hintze, the Foreign Secretary, to open peace negotiations through the Queen of the Netherlands. Even so, as long as her forces

continued to occupy large areas of Belgium and northern France, Germany might still hope to bargain from a position of some strategic strength. Ludendorff was therefore determined that, wherever possible, the existing front must be held. Influential German staff officers such as von Lossberg and von Kuhl believed that the most logical course was to withdraw, as in 1917, to a more defensible line behind the Somme but, for the moment, their arguments fell on deaf ears.

In stark contrast, the BEF's senior commanders were now much more flexible and receptive to sound tactical and strategic counsel from subordinates. In 1916 their response to stiffening opposition was often simply that of ordering repeated attacks in the same sector. Two years later, when German resistance increased at Amiens, Rawlinson heeded the advice of the Canadian Corps commander, Lieutenant-General Sir Arthur Currie, and recommended switching the point of the attack to the Third Army's front further north. If done soon, this would throw the Germans off balance, prevent them from concentrating reserves in one sector and deny them the time to establish new defences. Haig's support for these proposals signalled that the BEF was no longer invariably tempted to prolong offensives unnecessarily in the quest for a breakthrough and would henceforth inflict more significant damage on the Germans by unleashing a rolling series of attacks on different parts of the front. Foch initially wanted the British Fourth Army to continue battering the German positions east of Amiens but, by 15 August, he had allowed himself to be persuaded by Haig to accept Rawlinson's suggestions. The fact that Foch yielded relatively quickly to Haig's stand in this matter indicated that the BEF, in the latter half of 1918, was setting the pace of Allied operations. As the historians Robin Prior and Trevor Wilson have noted, this was also the last occasion on which Foch would attempt to issue orders to the British Commander-in-Chief.

The level of French performance in August was uneven though Mangin's Tenth Army was as vigorous as ever. After preparatory operations between Soissons and the Oise, Mangin's forces attacked northwards on 20 August, pushing on between two and three miles and capturing more than 8,000 prisoners from the German Ninth Army in the Battle of Noyon. Ludendorff saw this as 'another black day' of 'heavy and irreplaceable losses'. On 21 August, as decided the previous week, the BEF shifted the main weight of its own offensive to Byng's sector, between Arras and the old Somme battlefield. That day, the British Third Army pushed the Germans back around 4,000 yards and, on 22 August, Rawlinson's Fourth Army retook Albert. Haig, however, sensed that greater triumphs were within reach, calling for 'all ranks to act with the utmost boldness and resolution in order to get full advantage from the present favourable situation'. Spurred on by their Commander-in-Chief, the British Third and Fourth Armies renewed their attacks along a 33-mile front on 23 August. Three days later, the right wing of General Sir Henry Horne's First Army – to which the Canadian Corps had now returned – joined the offensive by assaulting the German defences east of Arras and south of the Scarpe.

Reeling from these successive attacks, Ludendorff was obliged to pull the Army Groups of von Boehn and Crown Prince Rupprecht back to an intermediate line running from the heights north-east of Noyon to the ground east of Bapaume, the latter town being re-entered by the New Zealand Division of Byng's Third Army on 29 August. Simultaneously the Germans abandoned their salient on the Lys in Flanders, surrendering much of the territory won during the *Georgette* offensive in April. Mount Kemmel passed back into British possession and by 4 September the Second and Fifth Armies had moved forward to a line stretching from Voormezeele in the north to Givenchy, near the La Bassée Canal.

The Dominion formations under Haig's command did not rest on their laurels, carrying out yet more outstanding operations as August gave way to September. In a brilliant feat of arms on 31 August and 1 September the 2nd Australian Division, under Major-General Rosenthal, stormed and held the formidable German bastion of Mont St Quentin, facilitating the capture of Péronne, the suburbs of which were cleared of Germans by midday on 2 September. That morning the Canadian Corps broke through the Drocourt-Quéant Position, or *Wotan Stellung*, south-east of Arras. As these vital points between the Somme and the Sensée fell in turn, Ludendorff's only option was to order a retirement to the Hindenburg Line – a course of action which Kuhl and Lossberg had advocated weeks before.

Closing up to the Hindenburg Line

In the first week of September, there were increasing signs that many German soldiers were rapidly losing confidence in their military leadership. Returning to the front from sick leave, Crown Prince Rupprecht recorded on 2 September that a troop train had been seen at Nuremberg bearing the inscription 'Slaughter cattle for Wilhelm and Sons! The German Army, nonetheless,

Australians of the 24th Battalion AIF photographed five minutes before they attacked at Mont St Quentin, 1 September 1918. (IWM)

remained a tough adversary and its front-line units still possessed sufficient collective tactical skill, patriotism and doggedness to exact a heavy toll in casualties for most local Allied successes. In the more fluid operations of August and September 1918, the Germans no longer relied principally upon linear trench systems – at least *not* west of the Hindenburg Line – and, during this phase of the fighting, machine-gunners provided the backbone of their resistance. All the same, as the BEF drew nearer to the outpost system of the Hindenburg Line, it faced the Alpine Corps and other formations which, because they were known to be dependable, were specially picked by the German High Command to hold these vital positions.

Between 4 and 26 September the BEF battled its way forward through the strong outpost defences around Epéhy and Havrincourt to secure a suitable jumping-off line for the coming assault on the main Hindenburg Line. Since 8 August, Haig's forces had driven the Germans back some 25 miles on a 40-mile front but had again paid a high price, the First, Third and Fourth Armies having together suffered nearly 190,000 casualties in this period. However, the gathering pace of the offensive – in marked contrast to the operations of 1916 and 1917 – and the growing feeling that victory might at last be in sight made such losses somehow easier to bear.

The historian Gregory Blaxland once remarked that, in the operations of the British First, Third and Fourth Armies during August and September, the Canadian and Australian Corps 'gored the German line like the horns of a bull, while the various British divisions, and one New Zealand, gave plenty of weight to the thrust of the forehead'. The outstanding deeds of the Australians and Canadians have, perhaps, been allowed to overshadow the invaluable, if often less spectacular, contribution of British divisions to the August–September operations. The élite German storm divisions in the March, April and May offensives had undoubtedly

Infantry of the 45th Battalion AIF following a creeping
barrage near Le Verguier, 18 September 1918. (IWM)

achieved brilliant initial progress but had
also invariably run out of steam after a few
days. From 8 August, on the other hand, the
majority of British divisions demonstrated
the ability to maintain a steady pressure on
the enemy for periods of up to six weeks.
This unrelenting pressure, made possible by
the British soldier's traditional powers of
endurance and sheer bloody-minded
persistence, ultimately counted far more
than dazzling breakthroughs in hastening
the Imperial German Army's downfall.

It must be remembered that, by this stage
of the war, most British infantry divisions
contained many inexperienced young
conscripts. However, co-operation between
infantry and gunners had vastly improved
since 1916 and the Royal Artillery was now
consistently capable of shepherding even the
greenest recruits towards their objectives
behind creeping barrages of immense power,
accuracy and depth. As officers at all levels
in the BEF were given additional

opportunities to display more imagination
and personal initiative in the semi-open
warfare of late 1918, so front-line troops
gained extra faith in their leaders. But
arguably the most important ingredient in
the BEF's new recipe for success was the
emphasis placed on teamwork and all-arms
co-operation. In its organisation and
infrastructure, its weapons and equipment,
and its tactics, the BEF now had a much
better overall balance than the German
Army and thus found it easier to adapt to
changing circumstances. Should one of its
arms fail in any given operation, a
combination of others could generally be
called upon to retrieve the situation and
ensure eventual success.

Foch, Haig and Pershing

Foch had sought, for some time, to widen
Allied offensive efforts. The plan he placed
before Pétain, Pershing and Haig on 24 July
was intended to eject the Germans from the
various salients created by their spring and

summer attacks and also to remove the German threat to the Paris–Nancy and Paris–Amiens railway communications. Considering Foch's long-held belief in the virtues of the offensive at all costs, these aims were comparatively modest, though he accepted Pershing's proposal that the recently-formed American First Army could reduce the potential menace to the Paris–Nancy railway by striking at the older German salient at St Mihiel. Early in August Foch was elevated to the rank of Marshal but, during that month, the amount of strategic and tactical co-ordination he actually attained fell far short of what was required of a Generalissimo. Of the French generals in the field, only the combative Mangin had yet inflicted significant damage on the Germans and the sluggish performance of Debeney – who commanded the French First Army on the British Fourth Army's right flank – drove Rawlinson to

distraction. In truth, Foch had so far failed to exert sufficient authority over Pétain in order to infuse the French armies with the necessary urgency and dynamism.

In this light, Foch was patently unfair in making repeated demands for the BEF to intensify its pressure on some of the toughest sectors of the entire Western Front, particularly as Haig's forces were currently bearing the largest, and most effective, share of Allied offensive operations. Haig was now using a headquarters train to shuttle him between the sectors where the BEF was most heavily engaged and had a much better 'feel' for the progress of the battle than he had possessed in earlier years. Sensing, perhaps more acutely than anyone, that victory might now be possible in 1918, Haig suggested to Foch, during the last week of August, that the

Foch and Pershing meet at Chaumont in the summer of 1918. (IWM)

Americans should be playing a bigger part in the ongoing offensive. The eradication of the St Mihiel salient was seen by Pershing and his staff as the precursor to a thrust eastward towards Metz. Haig, on the other hand, urged that more far-reaching results would be achieved if the Americans were to drive north-west, through the Argonne and Meuse valley, towards the railway hub of Mézières. An attack in this direction would converge with the BEF's own proposed push through and beyond the Hindenburg Line in the Cambrai-St Quentin area.

Foch had been thinking along similar lines for some days when Haig incorporated his advice in a letter to the Generalissimo on 27 August. Haig's arguments appear to have helped to crystallise Foch's strategy for, from this time onwards – under the slogan *Tout le monde à la bataille!* ('Everyone into battle!') – he clearly began to envisage operations which consisted of a rolling succession of brutal and interconnected blows with broader objectives than merely freeing railway centres or eliminating salients. Certainly, after an inconclusive and sometimes fractious meeting with Pershing on 30 August, Foch left a note with the American commander which mirrored Haig's ideas and proposed that all Allied forces should join 'in one great convergent attack'. Pershing understood the advantages of an attack towards Mézières but strenuously objected to Foch's suggestion that up to 16 American divisions should participate with the French Second and Fourth Armies in operations astride the Aisne and in the Meuse–Argonne region. He hastily reminded Foch that he could not back any plan that involved employing his formations piecemeal with other Allied armies. 'I do insist that the American Army must be employed as a whole ... and not four or five divisions here and six or seven there', he wrote on 31 August.

Two days later, after 'considerable sparring', Foch and Pershing reached a compromise. The attack at St Mihiel would go ahead first, but its objectives would be limited to the *Michel Stellung*, the German

defence line which stretched across the base of the salient. The American Expeditionary Force would then shift its main attention to the Meuse–Argonne sector where, under Pershing's command, it would play an appropriate role in the general Allied offensive. Having successfully stood his ground on the central issue, Pershing subsequently permitted *some* American divisions to serve with other Allied formations, such as the British Fourth Army, elsewhere on the Western Front.

St Mihiel

On 12 September, following a four-hour bombardment by 3,000 artillery pieces – mostly French, though half were fired by American gunners – seven American and two French divisions attacked the western and southern sides of the salient at St Mihiel. Other French formations assaulted the salient's 'nose'. Because of lapses in Allied security, the Germans were expecting an attack and had begun to pull back yet they could not prevent the AEF from registering a notable success in the first major American-led operation of the war. Within 30 hours, and at a cost of about 7,000 American casualties, Pershing's troops seized 460 German guns and 15,000 prisoners. No less impressive was the subsequent transfer of around 428,000 men and their equipment north-westwards to the Meuse–Argonne sector in under two weeks. The officer largely responsible for this remarkable feat of logistics was Colonel George C Marshall of the First Army's Operations Section – a future US Chief of Staff and Secretary of State.

As the detailed planning for the general Allied offensive on the Western Front was being completed, there were momentous developments in other theatres. In Palestine, Allenby's units had achieved a decisive breakthrough at Megiddo between 19 and 21 September, forcing the Turkish armies there into headlong retreat, while in Salonika the Bulgarians would shortly seek an armistice as a result of a vigorous

offensive which the Allies had launched
on 15 September. By the last week of the
month, the Allied commanders were ready to
initiate four separate but co-ordinated attacks
on the Western Front over a four-day period.
The first blow would be struck between
Reims and the Meuse by French and
American formations on 26 September. Next
day, 27 September, the British First and Third
Armies were to push towards Cambrai. On
28 September the rolling offensive would
extend to the extreme left flank, where an
attack between the Lys and the sea would be
opened by a composite Flanders Army
Group, commanded by Albert, King of the
Belgians, and comprising the Belgian Field
Army, 10 divisions of Plumer's British Second
Army and nine French divisions, three of
which were cavalry formations. Finally,

on 29 September, Rawlinson's British
Fourth Army, supported on its right by the
French First Army, was to assault the
Hindenburg Line near St Quentin.

Hammer blows

The opening blow of the general Allied
offensive – administered by the US First Army
and French Fourth Army in the Meuse–
Argonne region – had an immediate impact as
the Americans advanced up to three miles on
the first day. However, this rate of progress was
not maintained. The Germans had sited
defensive positions with their usual expertise
in the thickly-wooded and steeply-sloping
terrain between the Argonne Forest and the
Meuse. Supply problems quickly multiplied in

The final Allied offensive, September–November 1918

this testing countryside as Allied losses also grew. The undoubted courage of the American troops – like that of the British on the Somme in 1916 – could not always make up for their tactical naïveté or shortcomings in staff work. By the end of the month, after five days of hard fighting, the maximum penetration achieved by the Allies in the Meuse–Argonne sector was only about eight miles.

On 27 September it was the turn of the British First and Third Armies to strike west of Cambrai. The right-hand formation of Horne's First Army was the Canadian Corps, under Lieutenant-General Sir Arthur Currie. The Canadians faced the Canal du Nord, which had been under construction in 1914 and was still dry in parts. To make the most of one of these dry stretches and thus avoid the more difficult sector directly ahead, Currie secured the approval of Haig and a more lukewarm Horne for an audacious plan involving an initial side-step to the south and a crossing on a narrow 2,600-yard front. Once over the canal, the Canadians would then spread out fanwise in a north-easterly direction on a front of over 15,000 yards. Currie's gamble paid off handsomely as the First and Third Armies thrust forward six miles in two days. Thereafter, stiffer German opposition was encountered and hard fighting was required but the Canadian success on the Canal du Nord opened the way for a drive against Cambrai.

The start of the offensive in Flanders on 28 September was equally promising. The first day saw the Allies under King Albert break out of the old Ypres Salient, reclaim Passchendaele Ridge and pass beyond the limits of the BEF's advance of the previous year. On 29 September Plumer's units recaptured Messines Ridge and reached Warneton on the Lys. Further north the Belgians were now only two miles from Roulers. The Allies progressed approximately nine miles in this phase of operations in Flanders but then slowed down as German reserves arrived and the familiar problems of rain and mud returned. In these deteriorating conditions, the French and Belgians on the left were particularly

handicapped by the inadequacy of the arrangements made by King Albert's French Chief of Staff, General Degoutte, for transporting supplies across the broken and swampy landscape of the former Ypres Salient. On 2 October another glimpse of the future was offered by an air drop of 13 tons of rations to forward Belgian and French troops. However, the overriding need to establish better lines of communication and reorganise the supply services in the French and Belgian sectors compelled the Allies to suspend major offensive operations in Flanders between 5 and 14 October.

Through the Hindenburg Line

The British Fourth Army's great set-piece assault on the Hindenburg Line commenced on 29 September after a four-day preparatory bombardment by 1,637 guns and howitzers firing some 750,000 shells. The attack was launched along a 12-mile front between Vendhuille and St Quentin. Facing the IX Corps on the Fourth Army's right wing was an intimidating stretch of the St Quentin Canal, which here was about 35 feet wide and passed through steep-sided, almost vertical cuttings with banks up to 60 feet high. It was therefore decided to make the principal thrust further north, between Vendhuille and Bellicourt, where the canal ran underground in a tunnel. This important assault sector was entrusted to the experienced but tired Australian Corps, which had been temporarily combined with the untried US II Corps for this attack.

To the consternation of Rawlinson and Monash, the raw US 27th Division was unable to take three important German outposts in a preliminary operation on 27 September. Because it was feared that artillery fire might hit American troops who might still be holding forward positions, these strongpoints were left largely untouched for two days and, for the same reason, the 27th Division dispensed with a creeping barrage for the first 1,000 yards of its advance on 29 September itself. Thirty-four accompanying tanks were of little assistance, as 11 received direct hits and

British Mark V tanks, carrying 'cribs' for trench crossing, move forward to the Hindenburg Line, 29 September 1918. (IWM)

seven stuck in shell holes or trenches. Consequently, Major-General Gellibrand's 3rd Australian Division, which had been expected to take part in the exploitation rather than the assault phase, was drawn in to the ferocious struggle much sooner than planned. To the right, the American 30th Division achieved better early progress, seizing Bellicourt by noon, but did not properly mop up all the positions it had overrun. Hence, when the 5th Australian division tried to move through the Americans, it met heavy machine-gun fire from posts which the Americans had failed to clear, also becoming involved in a tough fight as it strove to push on, with the Americans, beyond Bellicourt and Nauroy. Though the Australians and Americans had advanced nearly 4,000 yards and now controlled the southern end of the canal tunnel, the day's results were less than had been hoped.

The situation was retrieved, somewhat unexpectedly, by the British IX Corps, under Lieutenant-General Sir Walter Braithwaite, on the right, and particularly by the Territorials of the unglamorous 46th (North Midland) Division under Major-General Boyd. For the canal crossing, meticulous yet ingenious preparations had been made by the corps and divisional commanders and their staffs, and included the provision of mud mats, collapsible boats, floating piers, lifelines and scaling ladders as well as 3,000 life jackets obtained from Channel steamers. On the day of the assault, screened by fog and a fast-paced creeping barrage, the 137th (Staffordshire) Brigade rushed the defences on the western bank near Bellenglise and the 1/6th North Staffords captured the bridge at Riqueval intact before the Germans could explode their demolition charges. By 3.30 pm all three brigades were not only across the canal but had captured the whole of the Hindenburg Main System on the 46th Division's sector. The 32nd Division then 'leapfrogged' through to continue the advance, consolidate the bridgehead and widen the breach along the eastern bank and the high ground to the south. When night fell IX Corps had

Brigadier-General J V Campbell VC addresses the
137th Brigade, 46th Division, from Riqueval Bridge,
2 October 1918. (IWM)

penetrated between three and four miles,
capturing the Hindenburg Main Position and
part of its Support Line. Fourth Army took
over 5,300 prisoners, with the 46th Division
alone seizing 4,200.

Despite the disappointing progress on the
left flank, the 46th Division's superb assault

had decisively ruptured the Hindenburg Line,
enabling the French First Army – whose attacks
had been frustratingly slow and half-hearted
on Rawlinson's right – to enter St Quentin
three days later. On 3 October another set-piece
assault by five divisions of Fourth Army tore
open a six-mile gap in the Hindenburg Reserve
Position or Beaurevoir Line, the rearmost
trenches and fortified positions of the great
Siegfried Stellung. The Australians, though now
exhausted, distinguished themselves yet again

in their final action on the Western Front, when three battalions of the 2nd Australian Division drove elements of at least four German divisions from the strongly-defended village of Montbréhain.

Pursuit

On 28 September, two days before Bulgaria became the first of Germany's allies to

conclude an armistice, Ludendorff told Hindenburg that Germany herself must follow suit without further delay. The leaders parted that evening 'like men who have buried their dearest hopes', Ludendorff wrote. They were disturbed to learn the next day that von Hintze had not yet acted upon the earlier proposal to make peace overtures through the Queen of the Netherlands. Even more upsetting was the Foreign Secretary's warning that revolution was inevitable if real parliamentary government was not immediately introduced. An emissary was sent to Berlin to inform the Reichstag of the current situation and, on 3 October, Prince Max von Baden, a liberal and known peace advocate, replaced von Hertling as Chancellor. Both Germany and Austria at once despatched peace notes to the United States. The Fourteen Points, a set of peace conditions that had been placed before the US Congress by President Woodrow Wilson in January, constituted a basis for subsequent negotiations yet, even at this late date, Hindenburg and Ludendorff sought to avoid ceding Alsace-Lorraine or any eastern territories they regarded as rightfully German.

The strength of German infantry formations in the field was now perilously low. Over 20 divisions were disbanded in an effort to maintain battalions at a strength of 450–550 but some could only muster 150 officers and men. German artillery units and machine-gunners were still fighting obstinately, however, and slowed the pace of the Allied advance. On 8 October the British Third and Fourth Armies, with Debeney's French First Army on their right, attacked along a 17-mile front extending south from Cambrai, moving forward four miles. Patrols from the Canadian Corps and the British 57th Division entered Cambrai itself early on 9 October but within another 48 hours the Germans had made a stand on the River Selle, near Le Cateau. Haig's forces were again compelled to pause while a fresh set-piece attack was prepared.

In Flanders the Allies had improved their communications sufficiently to resume their most northerly offensive on 14 October. The

A Canadian patrol enters Cambrai, 9 October 1918. (IWM)

French units in the Flanders Army Group did not perform well, the most effective blows being struck by the Belgians and the British Second Army. Uncharacteristically, Plumer deliberately disregarded orders which would have limited his contribution to that of flank protection and pressed on across the Lys. This helped the British Fifth Army, on his right, to liberate Lille on 17 October. The same day, the Belgians freed Ostend and Horne's British First Army, to the south, entered Douai. The Belgians recaptured Zeebrugge and Bruges on 19 October while Plumer's formations occupied Courtrai. The Allies were now nearing the Dutch frontier and the British Second Army had progressed eight miles in less than a week. Prince Max received a grave report from Crown Prince Rupprecht concerning the steep decline in the fighting spirit of German troops, who were surrendering in large numbers when faced with an Allied attack.

There was no consolation for Germany's leaders on the diplomatic front. President Wilson responded to the German peace note on 8 October, asserting that the first condition for any discussions would be for Germany to relinquish all occupied territory. The Germans signalled their willingness to comply but, on 14 October, Wilson added that submarine operations must be terminated and that the Allies would only negotiate with a democratic German government. Prince Max again declared that Germany would accept such terms but Wilson redoubled the pressure, demanding, on 23 October, what virtually amounted to Germany's *unconditional* surrender.

This was all too much for Ludendorff. On 24 October a telegram, bearing Hindenburg's signature yet probably drafted by Ludendorff, pronounced that Wilson's terms were unacceptable and that resistance should continue 'with all our strength'. Having lost touch with reality and the mood of the German people, Ludendorff could not withstand the angry reaction of the Reichstag when the text of the telegram was leaked. He resigned on 26 October and was succeeded by General Wilhelm Groener, though Hindenburg survived as Chief of the General Staff.

Private Frederick 'Fen' Noakes

Private (later Guardsman) Frederick Elias 'Fen' Noakes, a draper from Tunbridge Wells in Kent, was born on 27 January 1896 and made several attempts to join the Army between 1914 and 1917, always being rejected on medical grounds. As a youth he suffered badly from asthma and was, by his own admission, thin and 'weakly' with 'little physical strength'. When turned down yet again in 1916 a mixture of patriotism and fear of being thought a 'shirker' drove him to improve his fitness by using chest-expanders and taking long walks and cycle rides. He finally passed a medical board in May 1917 and was soon called up for military service in June, being posted to Windsor for training in a reserve formation of the Household Battalion. From then until 1919 he wrote regularly to his family. He saw action during both the German March offensive and the victorious Allied advance in 1918 and was wounded twice. Even allowing for wartime censorship, his articulate letters provide an interesting commentary on the war, containing not only reports on his own daily activities but also forthright views on wider political issues. In 1934 he collated and typed these letters and then, in 1952, used them as the basis for a privately printed memoir, *The Distant Drum*, in which he added many of the previously missing military and geographical details and included some mature reflections on his opinions as a young man. Together the letters and book offer a valuable glimpse into the last 18 months of the war and can be seen as an accurate barometer of the attitudes and morale of British soldiers on the Western Front in 1918.

Noakes crossed to France in November 1917, joining the Household Battalion – a unit of the 4th Division – in the Arras area. At this stage he still retained a 'credulous idealism', counting it 'an honour to take part in the most righteous war England ever waged, the Last Crusade ... Victory is in our grasp, and we should be utterly unworthy of the trust reposed in us if we turn back now.

Private (later Guardsman) F E 'Fen' Noakes. (IWM)

No *peace* until Prussian militarism is in *pieces'*. After a few weeks his views began to change. On 8 January 1918 he complained about the 'spirit of savagery' in the British press. 'Could the fighting men ... of both sides come together there can be no doubt that complete unanimity would result', he remarked. Noakes now felt that 'national pride', or obstinacy, 'will prove a great obstacle in the way of a reasonable settlement'. He called for a 'much greater openness of mind and humanity' lest Britain become infected with 'the very spirit of Prussianism we set out to crush'. By 12 February he was asking when 'all this indiscriminate murder' would cease. '*Everyone*, except the people in power', he wrote, 'is heartily sick of it ... There is not a man out here who would not make peace in a moment ...'. In later life, however, he declared that this was 'a temporary wave of disillusionment' which represented 'no more than the normal habit of grousing for which the British soldier is notorious'.

From the end of January until early March, Noakes suffered from a poisoned finger and leg sores and was hospitalised in February at Le Tréport, near Dieppe. During this period the Household Battalion was disbanded as part of the reorganisation of the BEF and, on recovery, Noakes was sent to the 3rd Coldstream Guards, then serving in the 4th Guards Brigade attached to the 31st Division. Between 23 and 25 March the battalion was in action near Ervillers, north of Bapaume, on the Third Army's front. Noakes recalled how tired he was following three days and nights without sleep. Eventually, as the German attacks grew heavier and more intense – and with the battalion in danger of being outflanked or surrounded – the order was given to retreat. Noakes, by then, had sunk into a mood of weary fatalism. 'I ran for some distance with the rest', he told his mother, 'and then, with a feeling of disgust for the whole job, I slowed down to a walk. I really didn't care which way things went'. He was, in fact, knocked unconscious and wounded in the forearm by a shell.

'Fen' Noakes spent over four months convalescing near Boulogne. The March crisis and the threat of defeat revived some of his former 'enthusiasm for the national cause' although 'my "patriotism" was never afterwards so unqualified and my devotion was more critical, than they had been in the past'. By 5 May he was again optimistic and commented with remarkable insight that 'I think we have got Fritz on the toasting-fork all right. He has made progress, but it has cost him far more casualties than he expected, and all the result has been is to put him in an impossible position. He is weakened out of all proportion to his gain, but he cannot stay where he is ...'

He returned to his unit in August but, towards the end of that month, was transferred to the 1st Battalion of the Coldstream Guards in the prestigious Guards Division. The Allied offensive had now been in progress for three weeks and Noakes was 'fairly certain that the war will be definitely decided, if not ended, before the winter'. In September, as the Guards Division advanced towards the Canal du Nord and Hindenburg Line, Noakes was struck, more than once, by the absence of Germans on his immediate front. On 13 September he recorded that men coming back from the forward positions were saying 'We can't find the enemy' or 'We've lost Fritz'. Noakes also noted that he had seen only three dead bodies and *no* wounded all day. 'I wish all battles were like that', he added. Noakes was profoundly impressed by the scale of the supporting barrage during the attack on the Canal du Nord on 27 September and, although he felt 'stark naked' when required to cross open ground under heavy fire, he also experienced 'an extraordinary sensation – curiously like relief – that I was no longer personally responsible for my own safety'. The attack was successful but Noakes and his comrades were too exhausted to care about their achievement: 'our mouths and throats were dry as lime-kilns. Nerves were on edge and tempers frayed as always after the intense strain of "going over the top" '. On 9 October, in another attack at Wambaix, near Cambrai, Noakes was wounded in the left leg. 'That was the end of the war, so far as my insignificant personal part in it went,' he recalled.

As the war drew to a close, Noakes was convalescing at a camp at Cayeux, near the mouth of the Somme. Attracted by the ideas of President Woodrow Wilson of the United States, Noakes was worried that Britain and France, in the elation of victory, would impose a vengeful settlement upon Germany. 'A lasting peace it must be,' he told his father, 'but it must also be an absolutely *clean* peace. Otherwise, the war has been in vain.' The announcement, on 11 November, that the Armistice had been signed was, however, 'a moment of such undiluted happiness and emotion as I had never known and probably shall never know again'.

Rejoicing in his new rank of 'Guardsman', Noakes served briefly with the British occupation forces in Cologne before coming home to England in March 1919. Demobilised in October that year, he returned to work in his family's drapery business. This sensitive and perceptive former soldier died, at the relatively young age of 57, on 12 April 1953.

The home fronts, 1917–1918

France

1917 was the year of maximum strain for France. With the Germans still on her soil, France continued to fight for her very existence although the fierce patriotism of 1914 had largely given way to weary resignation. While most French citizens were undoubtedly willing to carry on the struggle, they were, in some respects, less regimented or amenable to discipline than their British and German counterparts and the national mood was consequently more volatile. The malaise and restlessness which followed Verdun was heightened by the Russian Revolution and the failure of the Nivelle offensive, becoming manifest in increased anti-war activities and propaganda from pacifist and defeatist elements in French society. Even if the great mass of the French people refused to be seduced by such agitation, particularly after morale had been steadied by America's declaration of war on Germany, the number of strikes in French industry and public services rose alarmingly from 98 in 1915 to 689 in 1917.

Food shortages worsened in 1917. As less than one-third of French sugar factories remained operational, supplies of this commodity were especially meagre. Bread was coarser, regulated by size and weight and barely recognisable from the pre-war product. In January 1918 bread was rationed at 10 ounces per head per day, a severe blow to working people who relied heavily on this item of diet. Milk, butter and eggs too were scarce and expensive and, as the nation was forced to tighten its belt yet again in 1918, cafés and restaurants closed earlier than ever while butchers shut their shops up to three days a week. In May 1918 municipal butchers' shops were introduced in Paris to reduce and control meat prices. Despite such austerity and some temporary emergencies, France's food supplies were never so precarious as those of Britain and Germany and neither were her regulations and restrictions so stringent. However, manpower shortages on the home front were sufficiently serious – even allowing for the widespread employment of women – that, between April 1917 and January 1918, some 350,000 troops were withdrawn from the firing line to work on the land, in mines, on the railways and in education.

To add to their other trials, Parisians were subjected to heavy air raids by German Gotha bombers, 120 people being killed in March 1918 alone. As the German spring offensives brought the enemy closer to the capital than at any time since 1914, Paris was once more incorporated into the Zone of the Armies and could be reached by German long-range guns. From 23 March to 9 August 1918, Paris was shelled on 44 separate days and 256 citizens were killed. The menace ended when the Allied armies began to advance.

By then, France at last had more stable and energetic political leadership. In September 1917, the government of Alexandre Ribot collapsed following the earlier resignation of Louis-Jean Malvy, the radical Minister of the Interior whose laxity in suppressing pacifist agitation and personal links with a newspaper known to have received money from Germany eventually caused him to be charged with treason. Ribot's immediate successor as Prime Minister, Paul Painlevé, in turn gave way, on 16 November, to Georges Clemenceau. Though aged 76 when he took office, 'Tiger' Clemenceau – as he was nicknamed – shared President Poincaré's determination to wage war to the finish and possessed the charisma, courage and grip needed to command the nation's support. Merciless towards pacifists and defeatists, but also prepared to respond to reasonable industrial grievances, he did much to sustain French and Allied morale during the spring of 1918 and rallied his nation for one final effort that autumn.

Britain

Like France, Britain was showing increasing signs of war-weariness by 1917. There were 688 strikes and trade disputes during the year, involving 860,000 workers. Apart from the dilution of skilled labour by unskilled men and women, reported grievances included high prices, the unequal distribution of food, poor housing and restrictions on the mobility of workers. It must be stated, however, that industrial disputes were still fewer than in the immediate pre-war period and that even the widespread strikes in 1918 mostly occurred from July onwards, when the worst of the crises on the Western Front had passed. Most people, in fact, remained prepared to 'stick it out' until victory was assured.

As the historian Gerard DeGroot has observed, many of Britain's problems stemmed from a 'sometimes obsessive adherence to outdated values' and a lingering reluctance by the government to intervene. This even applied under the supposedly more dynamic Lloyd George. A case in point was the continuing inability to ensure a rational co-ordination of military and industrial manpower demands. A scheme launched in 1917 by the newly-established Department of National Service under Neville Chamberlain failed to achieve a more balanced allocation of manpower because it relied on voluntary enrolment for 'work of national importance' and lacked statutory obligation. An important step was taken in August 1917 when Auckland Geddes, formerly Director of Recruiting, succeeded Chamberlain as the head of a department that was accorded ministerial status and which, in November, took over control of recruiting from the War Office. From now on the Army's demands were, in the main, given a lower priority than

those of shipbuilding or aircraft and tank production. The Military Service (No.2) Act of April 1918 conscripted men aged 41 to 50 and also provided for the extension of compulsory service to Ireland although, wisely, the government never sought to enforce the latter. Temporary increases in enlistment totals were achieved in the summer of 1918 but came too late to prevent the reduction in the BEF's infantry battalions.

The huge part played by Britain's women in the national war effort was a crucial factor in helping the country to surmount such manpower difficulties. Over 7,310,000 women were in paid employment by July 1918. The 947,000 who worked in munitions production represented 90 per cent of that industry's workforce, while 117,000 were employed in transport and another 228,000 in agriculture – many in the Women's Land Army which came into being in 1917. Some donned uniforms in the new women's services, performing duties as cooks, clerks, mechanics and drivers to release men to fight. The Women's Army Auxiliary Corps – later called Queen Mary's Army Auxiliary Corps – was created in July 1917, followed by the Women's Royal Naval Service in November and the Women's Royal Air Force in April 1918. This vast and vital collective contribution was duly, if cautiously, acknowledged in the Representation of the People Act of February 1918, when women aged 30 or over were finally granted the vote.

Air attacks, particularly by Gotha bombers, caused renewed anxiety in 1917, the resulting outcry hastening the creation of the Royal Air Force as an independent service in April 1918. In all, 1,413 people were killed and 3,407 injured by air raids on Britain during the war. But the biggest threat to a nation dependent upon imports for its survival came with the unrestricted submarine campaign conducted by Germany from February 1917 onwards. In April 866,000 tons of British, Allied and neutral shipping were sunk, raising the spectre of starvation in Britain. The belated introduction of the convoy system in May, and the provision of air cover for convoys,

'For King and Country', by E F Skinner. (IWM)

substantially cut the loss rate but could not, by themselves, alleviate all Britain's food problems. Economy schemes promoted by the Food Controller, Lord Devonport, in February 1917, had proved ineffective as they were voluntary and falsely assumed that all members of the public shared the same sense of duty. The setting up of a Food Production Department of the Board of Agriculture was more successful in boosting domestic supplies, ultimately bringing 3,000,000 additional acres under cultivation. After Lord Rhondda had replaced Devonport at the Ministry of Food in April 1917, stricter controls were introduced and 15 Divisional Food Committees were empowered to regulate prices and distribution. Nevertheless, with shipping losses still higher in December than pre-1917 levels, more stringent measures could not be indefinitely delayed. In February 1918 compulsory rationing of several basic commodities was

blockade. For many Germans in the final 18 months of the war, the main diet consisted of adulterated bread, swedes or turnips and – when available – potatoes. Meat supplies were minimal and fats and eggs were hardly ever seen. In June 1918 citizens of Berlin were restricted to 1lb of potatoes each per week. Gnawing hunger was certainly the worst aspect of the daily ordeal on the German home front but it was not the only privation to be faced. There was little coal or other fuel for heating, lighting and transport. Closely linked with the shortages of coal and oil was the alarming deterioration of Germany's once-envied railway system, which now suffered from lack of maintenance of track and rolling-stock. Clothing too was scarce and, with shoe-leather almost unobtainable, many people now wore wooden-soled clogs.

One thing that was maintained was the Army High Command's iron grip on the direction of the national war effort. When the Chancellor, Bethmann-Hollweg, was manoeuvred from office in July 1917, he was replaced by the little-known and ostensibly subservient Georg Michaelis, who himself held the post for under four months. Michaelis lost the confidence of the Reichstag when he blamed the Social Democratic Party for a small but ominous mutiny among German sailors at Kiel, and he was compelled to resign. His successor was the elderly Bavarian Catholic Count Georg von Hertling, under whom political stability was restored and peace agitation was muffled, if not entirely silenced.

As in Britain and France, industrial unrest was an obvious symptom of war-weariness. In April 1917 a cut in the bread ration provoked strikes in Berlin and Leipzig. In the latter city the strikers called for a peace settlement without territorial annexations. In June strikers in the Ruhr demanded political reform. January 1918 saw more major industrial disputes in Berlin and Leipzig as well as in Essen and Hamburg. Again these strikes had a strong radical, almost revolutionary, flavour. On 1 February 1918 Berlin's seven biggest industrial plants were

instituted in London and the Home Counties and was extended throughout Britain in April. By July, thanks to rationing and the convoy system, the fear of starvation had largely vanished.

Germany

This could not be said of Germany, where domestic life was dominated by the ubiquitous and inescapable effects of the

A food queue in Britain. (IWM)

placed under martial law and a 'state of siege' was proclaimed for the capital. The ruthless mobilisation of the German economy and society under the Auxiliary Service Law and Hindenburg Programme squeezed the last ounce of productive effort out of the increasingly-regimented German people but the apparent success of the measures probably owed less to efficiency than to Germany's heightened siege mentality, which stiffened the resolve of most citizens not to yield so long as the Army remained unbeaten. Nevertheless, national morale – though briefly lifted by the transitory achievements of Ludendorff's 1918 offensives – undeniably became more brittle under the pressure of relentless physical privation. When it shattered the effects would be irreversible. It has frequently been claimed that Germany's defeat in the field followed a collapse on the home front, yet one can argue that Germany's final and sudden slide into chaos and revolution only gathered unstoppable momentum once the Hindenburg Line was threatened.

Caroline Webb

By November 1918 some 947,000 British women were engaged in munitions production. They included Caroline Webb, a 19-year-old girl from Camberwell in South London. Born on 24 January 1899, she was employed in a shirt factory in Bermondsey early in the war before switching to munitions work at Slade Green, near Dartford in Kent, where she filled trench mortar projectiles. Her basic wage at Slade Green was around 30 shillings a week, though she received an allowance of five shillings to cover her train fares from London Bridge. She could also earn a five-shilling bonus if she filled 60 projectiles in a nine-hour working day which started at 7.30 am.

The work was not without its dangers. Like many other women employed in shell-filling factories, she risked poisoning from long exposure to TNT (trinitrotoluene) and experienced the yellow skin discoloration that caused such women to be nicknamed 'canaries'. This could have unexpected advantages. As Caroline recalled in an oral history interview recorded for the Imperial War Museum in 1975, sympathetic railway employees would sometimes permit the women to travel in first class carriages. Others, however, 'used to treat us as though we was [the] scum of the earth … These old conductors used to say in the train "You'll die in two years, cock" … So we said "Well, we don't mind dying for our country."' Caroline was indeed so patriotic that she frequently spent a high proportion of her wages on parcels of chocolate, chewing gum and cigarettes for soldiers. 'I came out of the war with hardly a penny', she confirmed, 'and I thought "Thank God my conscience is clear."'

In 1917 Caroline left Slade Green to work at Woolwich Arsenal, her new job being to fill bullets with lead. Her pay increased to £2 10s per week but her working day now lasted 12 hours, from 7.00 am to 7.00 pm, over a 13-day period. After one day off, she would then work for 13 nights, again on a 12-hour shift. Not surprisingly – given that her sleep was often spoiled by air raids – she rarely went out on her rest day, describing herself as a 'proper old stop-at-home'. Caroline sometimes accompanied groups of girls from Woolwich Arsenal to indulge in a little mild flirtation with soldiers in nearby Beresford Square, although, in her case, flirting was all that occurred. She was not alone, in 1917–1918, in thinking that 'it was disgusting for girls to be pregnant' but many female workers at Woolwich did succumb to temptation. 'A lot of these poor kids came from up north', Caroline asserted, '… and they were more simple Simons'. Occasional pay cuts made her more militant, prompting her to join a trade union.

When the war ended, Caroline Webb was in no mood to celebrate. Her beloved father, one of the countless victims of the Spanish influenza pandemic, died two days before the Armistice. Caroline and her 47-year-old mother – who had recently had another baby – had to register the death on 11 November and were barely aware of outside events. When they heard maroons signalling the Armistice, 'we thought it was another air raid', Caroline admitted.

After the war, Caroline married, becoming Mrs Rennles. She and her husband – himself a former soldier – possessed little money at first and soon had a child. Caroline had even bought the boots which her husband wore on their wedding day. Bitter about being thrown 'on the slag heap', she took part in a protest march to Westminster that was dispersed by mounted police. Nevertheless, she was still working at the age of 76, running a shop in Coldharbour Lane, Brixton. She died in 1985. Her recorded reminiscences remain as testimony to the part which she, and nearly a million other British 'munitionettes' played in ensuring an Allied victory.

Caroline Webb (later Mrs Rennles). (IWM)

The final month

In presenting his peace conditions to Germany, President Wilson did not always fully consult his allies and some leading players felt that the terms might be too harsh. Haig, for one, prophetically remarked to his wife that Allied statesmen should 'not attempt to so humiliate Germany as to produce a desire for revenge in years to come'. Haig was particularly anxious to seek victory in 1918. He knew that the BEF was battle-weary and short of reinforcements, that the French Army probably lacked the capacity to mount a decisive offensive by itself and that the Americans were still not totally combat-hardened. Even so, he wished to deny the Germans any opportunity of establishing a new defensive line during the winter and, while hoping that moderate armistice terms might induce the Germans to capitulate, he simultaneously strove to keep the enemy off balance and moving backwards.

To this end, Rawlinson's Fourth Army struck the German positions on the Selle on 17 October. The main objective was a line from the Sambre and Oise Canal to Valenciennes, which would bring the Allies within artillery range of Aulnoye – a communications centre where the Mézières–Hirson railway joined that which stretched back to Germany through Maubeuge and Charleroi. Rawlinson's units, attacking on a ten-mile front south of Le Cateau, forced the passage of the Selle despite strong German opposition and, although the advance subsequently slowed, the Fourth Army's right wing managed to push forward around five miles to the Sambre Canal by the evening of 19 October. Horne's First Army also gained some six miles, bringing it level with the Third Army so that a joint night attack could be made across the Selle, *north* of Le Cateau, early on 20 October. As on other sectors, dogged resistance from their rearguards won the Germans enough breathing-space to bolster their defences east of the river with wire entanglements and the British First and Third Armies needed all day to move two miles and reach their immediate objectives. Determined not to let the enemy off the hook, Haig launched yet another combined night attack – by the First, Third *and* Fourth Armies – on 23 October, driving on six miles in two days. Further north, the Second and Fifth Armies were approaching the line of the Schelde. However, a pause was now required so that the next round of Allied attacks could be properly co-ordinated. Strategically, October had been a productive month for the BEF but, since breaking the Hindenburg Line, Haig's formations had, perhaps, met stiffer opposition than anticipated, suffering 120,000 casualties for an overall gain of approximately 20 miles.

Unknown to the front-line troops of both sides, the war now had less than two weeks to run. Following more than a month of fierce fighting in the Meuse-Argonne region, the US First Army breached the last significant German defence line on 1 November and, two days later, cut the crucial Lille-Metz railway. In the BEF's zone of operations, the Canadians took Valenciennes on 2 November preparatory to the larger set-piece assault on 4 November by the First, Third and Fourth Armies. This attack, supported by just 37 tanks, was delivered on a 30-mile front from Valenciennes to the River Sambre, on both sides of the Mormal Forest. In an almost symbolic minor operation that day, men of the New Zealand Division bravely scaled the ramparts of the walled town of Le Quesnoy to avoid a protracted siege and hasten the surrender of the garrison.

For the Central Powers the situation was beyond recovery. Turkey had already signed

Winston Churchill, the Minister of Munitions, at a march past of the British 47th Division at Lille, 28 October 1918. In front of him is Lieutenant-Colonel B L Montgomery, the division's Chief of Staff. (IWM)

an armistice with the Allies on 30 October and Austria-Hungary followed on 3 November. Sailors of the German High Seas Fleet, when ordered to put to sea for a pointless last sortie, mutinied on 29–30 October. By the evening of 4 November, Kiel was controlled by the mutineers and revolution was spreading inexorably throughout Germany. On Thursday 7 November a Bavarian Republic was declared in Munich, a few hours before a German delegation crossed the front lines to negotiate an armistice with Foch.

Even at this point the Allies did not relax the pressure. By 9 November, a Saturday, French forces were closing in on Mézières and two American corps gained the heights overlooking Sedan. On the opposite, or northern, flank the Allies were across the Schelde as the Germans pulled back to the Antwerp–Meuse line. The British Second Army

was now nearly 50 miles from its fields of sacrifice in the Ypres Salient. That day, Prince Max prematurely announced that the Kaiser had abdicated and, after a German Republic had been proclaimed from the Reichstag, the only course left for Wilhelm II was to relinquish the throne and escape to exile in Holland. Around 5.00 am on 11 November, the Armistice was signed in a railway coach of Foch's special train at Rethondes in the Forest of Compiègne. During the morning Canadian troops appropriately entered Mons, the scene of the BEF's first battle of the war. Then, at 11.00 am, after 1,568 days of conflict, the guns at last fell silent and the long agony of the Western Front was ended.

Counting the cost

The crushing victories of the final Allied advance were won at a heavy cost. In the 'Hundred Days' campaign between August and November, the BEF incurred some 350,000 casualties – more than it had suffered during the Third Battle of Ypres. Its daily casualty rate in this period (3,645) was higher than that on the Somme in 1916. In the Meuse-Argonne fighting, the Americans too lost 117,000 men in 47 days.

The precise cost of the First World War, in terms of human lives, will probably never be known. German losses numbered at least 1,808,545 dead and 4,247,143 wounded, while French casualties have been estimated at nearly 5,000,000, of whom 1,385,300 were dead or missing. One hundred and fifteen thousand, six hundred and sixty Americans lost their lives out of overall casualty figures of 325,876. The total losses of the British Empire were 3,260,581, including 947,023 dead and missing. On the Western Front alone, British and Dominion casualties were 2,690,054. Of these 677,515 officers and other ranks were killed, died of their wounds or went missing and a further 1,837,613 suffered non-fatal wounds.

A little over 12 per cent of the total number of British soldiers who served in France and Belgium were killed or died and almost 38 per cent were wounded. Thus about half of the BEF's soldiers on the Western Front would expect to become casualties, some more than once. Approximately one in eight would be killed. The BEF's non-battle casualties, from sickness and accidental injuries, amounted to 3,528,468 officers and men. Of these 32,098 died from a variety of causes, including pneumonia, frostbite and meningitis. It is a tribute to the BEF's medical services, however, that around 80 per cent of wounded soldiers who passed through their hands not only recovered but even returned to some form of duty. One should also note that world-wide mortalities from the Spanish influenza pandemic of 1918–1919 may have reached 20,000,000 – more than were killed in the war.

Crowds outside Buckingham Palace on Armistice Day, 11 November 1918. (IWM)

The Ossuary and French national war cemetery at Douaumont, Verdun. (AKG Berlin)

Since over 80 per cent of those who served in the BEF survived the conflict – albeit with severe wounds, lost limbs or deep psychological scars – it is misleading to talk or write of a 'Lost Generation'. On the other hand, as the work of Dr J M Winter has shown, over 70 per cent of British soldiers who died were under the age of 30. Moreover, the *proportion* of fatal casualties was higher among junior officers than among other ranks and, because many such officers came from middle-

and upper-class families, and had attended public schools and universities, one could claim that a disproportionate share of the sacrifice was borne by one generation of these particular social groups. However, the war memorials which are still so evident in cities, towns and villages throughout Britain and the Commonwealth or France, for example, serve as a silent but powerful reminder that few communities and families among the belligerent nations were left untouched by the war's demands and tragedies.

Very little was truly solved by the peace settlement imposed by the Treaty of Versailles

by Allied forces for five, 10 and 15 years. Germany was also called upon to pay reparations – principally to France and Britain – though the amounts to be found were not specified until the early 1920s. In the event, by the time the reparations were terminated in 1932, Germany had paid less than half the sum set a decade or so earlier, the victors of Versailles having lacked the political will or military muscle to extract the full amount. Moreover, if Germany was forbidden by the Versailles settlement to maintain a large conscript army or possess offensive weapons such as submarines, battleships and aircraft, the Treaty did not dismember the country nor did it deprive Germany of the industrial complex upon which her war machine had hitherto been based. On the other hand, reparations almost certainly helped to undermine the post-war German economy and, together with the attribution of 'war guilt' to Germany under Article 231 of the Treaty, sowed the seeds of resentment which were only too eagerly exploited by Hitler and the Nazis in the 1920s and early 1930s. The latter chose to ignore the inconvenient detail that the German Army was essentially beaten in the field by November 1918 and would have unquestionably suffered an even more humiliating defeat the following year. Indeed, they used the fact that the German Army was still in action on the Western Front when the Armistice was signed as an excuse to nurture the myth that domestic collapse had constituted a 'stab in the back' and betrayed the country's fighting men.

International stability was not enhanced by the creation of new states – such as Czechoslovakia and Yugoslavia – in central, eastern and southern Europe which would themselves contain frustrated national or ethnic minorities. The establishment of a League of Nations represented a laudable effort to ensure that international disputes would henceforth be settled without recourse to war. Unfortunately, the attempt failed largely because of the non-participation of its main proponent – the United States Senate having declined to ratify the settlement on the grounds that it

of 28 June 1919. Professor Ian Beckett describes the Treaty as being, in some respects, 'an unhappy compromise between the French desire for a punitive settlement, the British desire for stability and the American desire to create a better world based on principles of internationalism, democracy and self-determination'. It did *not* fail, as has so often been argued, because its terms were too severe. Germany had to return Alsace-Lorraine to France and give up conquered territories inhabited primarily by non-German peoples, while the Rhineland was divided into three zones which were to be occupied respectively would infringe national sovereignty. In Britain and France, war-weariness, emphasised by the literature of disillusionment in the late 1920s and early 1930s and intensified by economic slump and mass unemployment, encouraged appeasement and weakened national resolve to resist Hitler's ambitions until it was too late to prevent another cataclysmic conflict.

The real or perceived shortcomings of the Versailles peace settlement and the convulsion of the Second World War have undoubtedly obscured the nature and scale of the Allied triumph on the Western Front in 1918. As John Terraine has tirelessly pointed out, the final 'Hundred Days' campaign of August–November 1918 was the only time when the British Army has defeated the main body of the principal enemy in a continental war. From tiny beginnings the BEF grew into what was arguably the nation's biggest-ever enterprise and by 1918 was a modern, all-arms force employing tanks, ground-attack aircraft, armoured cars, motorised machine-gun units, air supply by parachute and signals deception. Given their lack of preparation before 1914, both the victory of 1918 and the manner in which it was won were – for Britain and the Dominions – colossal achievements.

Further reading

Asprey, R., *The German High Command at War: Hindenburg and Ludendorff and the First World War*, William Morrow, London, 1991.

Bean, C.E.W., *Official History of Australia in the War of 1914–18: The Australian Imperial Force in France (1916–1918), Volumes III–VI*, Angus and Robertson, Sydney, 1929–1942.

Beckett, I.F.W., *The Great War 1914–1918*, Longman, London, 2001.

Blaxland, G., *Amiens 1918*, Frederick Muller, London, 1968.

Bond, B. and Cave, N., (eds) *Haig: A Reappraisal 70 Years On*, Leo Cooper/Pen and Sword, Barnsley, 1999.

DeGroot, G., *Blighty: British Society in the era of the Great War*, Longman, London, 1996.

Edmonds, Brigadier-General Sir J.E. (with Falls, Captain C. and Miles, Captain W.), *Official History of the War: Military Operations, France and Belgium, 1917 (Volumes I–III) and 1918 (Volumes I–V)*, Macmillan and HMSO, London, 1935–1948.

Griffith, P., *Battle Tactics of the Western Front: The British Army's Art of Attack, 1916–18*, Yale University Press, London, 1994.

Gudmundsson, B., *Stormtroop Tactics: Innovation in the German Army, 1914–1918*, Praeger, New York, 1989.

Harris, J.P. and Barr, N., *Amiens to the Armistice: The BEF in the Hundred Days' Campaign, 8 August–11 November 1918*, Brassey's, London, 1998.

Nicholls, J., *Cheerful Sacrifice: The Battle of Arras 1917*, Leo Cooper, London, 1990.

Passingham, I., *Pillars of Fire: The Battle of Messines Ridge, June 1917*, Sutton Publishing, Stroud, 1998.

Pedersen, P., *Monash as Military Commander*, Melbourne University Press, 1985.

Philpott, W., *Anglo-French Relations and Strategy on the Western Front, 1914–18*, Macmillan, London, 1996.

Prior, R. and Wilson, T., *Passchendaele: The Untold Story*, Yale University Press, London, 1996.

Rawling, B., *Surviving Trench Warfare: Technology and the Canadian Corps, 1914–1918*, University of Toronto Press, 1992.

Schreiber, S., *Shock Army of the British Empire: The Canadian Corps in the last 100 Days of the Great War*, Praeger, Westport, CT, 1997.

Sheffield, G., *Forgotten Victory: The First World War, Myths and Realities*, Headline, London, 2001.

Smith, L., *Between Mutiny and Obedience: The Case of the French Fifth Infantry Division during World War I*, Princeton University Press, New Jersey, 1994.

Terraine, J., *To Win a War: 1918, The Year of Victory*, Sidgwick and Jackson, London, 1978.

Travers, T., *How the War was Won: Command and Technology in the British Army on the Western Front, 1917–1918*, Routledge, London, 1992.

Walker, J., *The Blood Tub: General Gough and the Battle of Bullecourt, 1917*, Spellmount, Staplehurst, 1998.

Williams, J., *The Home Fronts: Britain, France and Germany, 1914–1918*, Constable, London, 1972.

Index

Related titles & companion series from Osprey

ESSENTIAL HISTORIES (ESS)
**Concise overviews of major wars
and theatres of war**

CAMPAIGN (CAM)
**Strategies, tactics and battle experiences
of opposing armies**

MEN-AT-ARMS (MAA)
**Uniforms, equipment, history
and organisation of troops**

WARRIOR (WAR)
**Motivation, training, combat experiences
and equipment of individual soldiers**

ELITE (ELI)
**Uniforms, equipment, tactics and personalities
of troops and commanders**

ORDER OF BATTLE (OOB)
**Unit-by-unit troop movements and
command strategies of major battles**
Contact us for more details – see below

NEW VANGUARD (NVG)
**Design, development and operation
of the machinery of war**

AIRCRAFT OF THE ACES (ACES)
**Experiences and achievements
of 'ace' fighter pilots**

AVIATION ELITE (AEU)
Combat histories of fighter or bomber units
Contact us for more details – see below

COMBAT AIRCRAFT (COM)
**History, technology and crews
of military aircraft**
Contact us for more details – see below

To order any of these titles, or for more information on Osprey Publishing, contact:
Osprey Direct (UK)   *Tel:* +44 (0)1933 443863   *Fax:* +44 (0)1933 443849   *E-mail:* info@ospreydirect.co.uk
Osprey Direct (USA) c/o MBI Publishing   *Toll-free:* 1 800 826 6600   *Phone:* 1 715 294 3345
Fax: 1 715 294 4448   *E-mail:* info@ospreydirectusa.com
www.ospreypublishing.com

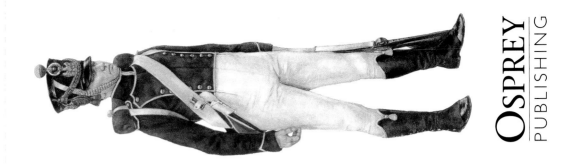

FIND OUT MORE ABOUT OSPREY

❏ Please send me a FREE trial issue of Osprey Military Journal

❏ Please send me the latest listing of Osprey's publications

❏ I would like to subscribe to Osprey's e-mail newsletter

Title/rank

Name

Address

Postcode/zip

State/country

E-mail

Which book did this card come from?

❏ I am interested in military history

My preferred period of military history is_____

❏ I am interested in military aviation

My preferred period of military aviation is _____

I am interested in *(please tick all that apply)*

❏ general history   ❏ militaria   ❏ model making

❏ wargaming   ❏ re-enactment

Please send to:

USA & Canada:
Osprey Direct USA, c/o MBI Publishing,
PO Box 1, 729 Prospect Ave, Osceola, WI 54020, USA

UK, Europe and rest of world:
Osprey Direct UK, PO Box 140, Wellingborough,
Northants, NN8 2FA, United Kingdom

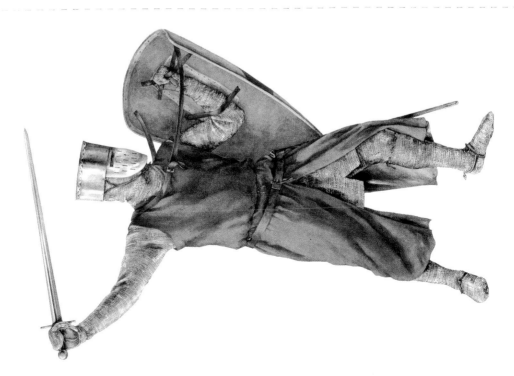

www.ospreypublishing.com

call our telephone hotline
for a free information pack

USA & Canada: 1-800-826-6600
UK, Europe and rest of world call:
+44 (0) 1933 443 863

Young Guardsman
Figure taken from *Warrior 22:
Imperial Guardsman 1799–1815*
Published by Osprey
Illustrated by Christa Hook

Knight, c.1190
Figure taken from *Warrior 1: Norman Knight 950 – 1204AD*
Published by Osprey
Illustrated by Christa Hook

POSTCARD